FOR THE LOVE OF GOOD FOOD

FOR THE LOVE OF MY LIFE, HUGH

BY THE SAME AUTHOR
· MADE IN INDIA ·

FRESH INDIA

MEERA SODHA

130 QUICK, EASY AND DELICIOUS
VEGETARIAN RECIPES FOR EVERY DAY

PHOTOGRAPHY BY DAVID LOFTUS

PENGUIN

FIG TREE

CONTENTS

ALTERNATIVE CONTENTS

SEASONAL CONTENTS

Due to innovations in the way we grow, transport and store food, we can now get most things the whole year round, which has obvious benefits. But this can also take away the enormous pleasure of eating something when nature says it is in its prime. And every now and then, when you buy out of season, you can end up with something rather tasteless that you wish you'd never bought in the first place.

Eating seasonally often feels exactly right. Broad beans, peas and asparagus taste perfect in spring when the promise of summer and sunshine is just round the corner. Big brutish roots, at their best after the first frosts, are great in curries or mashed up with spices, and feel comforting in the winter. With that in mind, here are some dishes to eat with the seasons.

EVERY RECIPE TELLS A STORY

At the heart of every one of my recipes is a place called Gujarat. It's where, as long as anyone can remember, our family came from. And although my family has now settled in England, we are still Gujarati, and day in day out we talk, think and eat like Gujaratis.

Gujarat, a small state on the western coast of India, has had a very big impact on Indian food culture. It all started in 269BC when Emperor Ashoka banned the slaughter of any living animal in the name of peace. Since that time, the majority of the millions of Hindus in the state have been vegetarian. Over thousands of years, a rich and resourceful vegetable-first way of cooking has evolved. Home cooks, restaurant chefs and street-food stallholders alike have all been creating simple but extraordinary dishes, using just what grows on the land and is in season.

Walk the streets of Ahmedabad or Rajkot and you'll come across simple but heavenly potato curries cooked with garlic, mustard seeds and tomatoes. Or sweetcorn cooked in a deeply savoury sauce of ground peanuts and yoghurt and aubergines that have been smoked over red coals until they become deeply mysterious and creamy.

I've long been fascinated by how this limitation of not cooking with meat has been the catalyst for new ways of thinking about and cooking with often familiar ingredients. Take the humble chickpea, for example. In Gujarati hands it has been transformed into a variety of dishes of different textures and forms – from the gossamer-like chickpea bread dhokla, studded with sesame and mustard seeds, to a silken handkerchief-like pasta called khandvi and even a meltingly soft fudge.

This is the Gujarati way: creative, fresh, and always vegetable first.

Although Gujarat in particular is famous for this, a similar story exists all across India. For hundreds of millions of people in India, vegetarianism is not a choice but a way of life.

I grew up here in England in a small farming village in Lincolnshire. Behind our house were fields bursting with potatoes, leeks, corn and chard, and down the road, rapeseed, mustard, cauliflower and all sorts of greens. Mum adopted and adapted, spicing all this produce to make our very own special dishes, from courgette kofta to runner bean bhajis, rhubarb chutney and even rainbow chard saag. With every dish, you could see the Gujarati resourcefulness and creativity at work.

When I moved from our little village to London twelve years ago, I continued to cook in much the same way as my mum had. As the years passed, I began to notice how my family's approach to cooking was so at odds with how most people thought about and experienced Indian food. While my family gravitated towards the fresh, the vibrant and the seasonal, Indian food in the UK was often heavy, swimming in brown sauce and lacking in variety.

I've written *Fresh India* to follow *Made in India* because I want to show you another type of Indian food, one that is vegetable led and packed with bold flavours. This is the food I love, which is influenced by how Gujaratis think about food but also by each and every state of India and occasionally Sri Lanka too.

Some of the dishes in *Fresh India* have been passed down the generations in my family and haven't seen the light of day outside our home until now. Many have come from my travels all over India and the people I have met along the way, from home cooks to street stall vendors, temple cooks to chefs in top restaurants.

Others have come from my experiments in the kitchen, taking classic Indian techniques and flavours and imagining something new. After all, I'm sure I'm not the only one who has wondered what an Indian salad could look and taste like.

This is a book all about vegetables, but whether you call it a vegetarian cookbook is up to you. I'm aware I've written it at a time when a change is taking place in our attitudes towards both meat and vegetables. More of us are questioning how we farm, how we treat animals and whether how we eat is sustainable, good for the environment and also for our health.

But my aim with this book is not to preach or to write only for vegetarians: it is to inspire you to cook a different, fresher, vegetable-led type of Indian food. To honour the seasons and what grows in our fields, and also to celebrate the way that hundreds of millions of Indians eat, and the Gujarati way of thinking.

Happy cooking.

Meera x

HELPFUL WEIGHTS + MEASURES

Ingredients vary in size and potency, but this is a good rough guide if you're substituting whole spices for ground, scaling up recipes or don't have a pair of scales to hand.

GENERAL

1 teaspoon = ⅓ of a tablespoon = 5ml

1 tablespoon = 3 teaspoons = 15ml

RICE + PULSES

Appetites will vary (so plan accordingly), but as a general rule allocate 65g of dry rice per person. As for pulses, allow 100g of the dried variety per person, or 200g of cooked.

SPICES

You might find the following measures helpful if grinding whole spices:

BLACK PEPPER   1 teaspoon of peppercorns = 1½ teaspoons of ground pepper

CARDAMOM   Approximately 12 pods = 1 teaspoon of ground cardamom

CORIANDER   1 teaspoon of coriander seeds = 1¼ teaspoons of ground coriander

CUMIN   1 teaspoon of cumin seeds = 1¼ teaspoons of ground cumin

FENNEL   1 teaspoon of fennel seeds = 1¼ teaspoons of ground fennel

MUSTARD SEEDS   1 teaspoon of mustard seeds = 1½ teaspoons of ground mustard

NUTMEG   ½ a nutmeg = 1 teaspoon of ground nutmeg

CITRUS FRUIT

1 lime = roughly 30ml or 2 tablespoons of juice
I lemon = roughly 50ml or 3 tablespoons of juice

GARLIC

1 fat clove of garlic = 1 teaspoon of finely chopped garlic

ONIONS

1 large brown onion = approximately 200g

HOW TO USE THIS BOOK

Traditionally, Indians eat a couple of different dishes for lunch or dinner. Dotted around the table you might find one or two curries, a dal, some rice and maybe a pile of chapattis. If you're lucky, you'll also get a tray of chutneys and a side of raita too. We tend to focus the meal not on one central 'hero' dish, but around a few smaller ones, so you get a lot more flavour and texture.

This wonderfully varied way of eating has evolved over many centuries, and has in part been made possible by the amount of time Indian women have spent in the kitchen. But given our busy lifestyles, we all like a bit of simplicity when it comes to cooking during the week, which might mean a one-pot dish cooked in half an hour or making something in the same time it would take to order a takeaway. So I've written this book in a way that will satisfy different levels of time and enthusiasm. You can either combine a few different dishes or just cook one thing for dinner.

There are no rules, but I've made some suggestions in the introductions to each chapter, or under the recipes themselves, for what will go with what. Where you see 'Serves 4 as a main course' you shouldn't need anything else alongside except some rice or bread, but where you see 'Serves 4 as part of a main course' you might want another dish to go with it.

When I'm cooking during the week, I'll often cook a standalone dish, like a rice packed with vegetables, or a curry, soaking the rice before I start cooking. In the fridge I'll always have a few different pickles and some yoghurt to make raita with. But when the weekend hits, I love to take my time and make a couple of things, or cook a big batch of dal to last a few days.

With any cuisine, the big question is always how to hang it all together so it makes sense. For that reason I've included a few menu suggestions, which you'll find on page 208.

I've also included symbols for all gluten-free, dairy-free and vegan recipes, which are marked on each page with the abbreviations shown to the left.

 GLUTEN-FREE

 DAIRY-FREE

 VEGAN

TEN WAYS TO

RAISE YOUR GAME

IN THE KITCHEN

01
TASTE AS YOU GO

Taste as you go, from beginning to middle to end. This is the simplest but best piece of advice my mother ever gave me. That way you'll learn what you like and what you don't. It will also give you a better understanding of the personalities of the ingredients you're dealing with and how they change with time, heat and when mixed with other things. Soon you'll be able to create great food without a recipe.

02
GET SOME BALANCE

Most Indian home cooking is balanced. One ingredient shouldn't be vying for your attention more than any other. Often people think chilli should be the hero, but that's rarely true, and especially not when it comes to fresh vegetables. Let them take centre stage and allow the other ingredients to act as backing vocals.

03
NOT ALL CHILLIES
ARE CREATED EQUAL

Chillies and chilli powders vary hugely in potency. I (almost) always use the same slim green finger chillies bought from Ali the Bengali on Chapel Market, and buy the same brand of chilli powder too. I've got to know my chillies and spices intimately so there are never any nasty surprises and I can judge how much to use.

04
ALWAYS WASH YOUR RICE

Washing rice helps to remove a lot of the starch that can make rice sticky and, at worst, gloopy. The best way to wash your rice is to put it in a bowl and pour water over it. Swirl it around and tip out the starchy water, repeat until the water runs clear, then pour in fresh water to soak – 30 minutes in cold water is perfect, but 10 minutes in warm water is fine if you don't have that long. If you wash your rice through a sieve it's not as easy to tell how 'clean' it is. Washing and soaking rice is the first thing I do in the kitchen before cooking, so I can have dinner and rice ready at the same time.

05
COOK YOUR ONIONS FOR
AS LONG AS POSSIBLE

Make sure you cook your onions for long enough. Try taking things a little further next time you cook them (without burning them) and you'll see what I mean. They are in so many recipes, and it makes all the difference.

06
EMBRACE FAILURE

With Indian food, if you go too far with one ingredient or another, you can usually recover. Too much chilli or salt? Add tomatoes or coconut or double the recipe to dilute it. Or embrace messing up: chefs say this a lot, but it is true – don't worry if you mess up, as you'll learn from it.

07
PRACTICE MAKES PERFECT

These days we expect to dip into any cookery book, from Korean food to Georgian, and be able to cook something perfectly first time around. The truth is that sometimes it takes a while to build up proper skills. I've now been making chapattis for years, but initially they were wonky. Over time my hands found a rhythm with the rolling pin and I got a feel for the dough, and now my chapattis are both round and pillow soft, like my mum's. If at first things aren't perfect, keep going.

08
GROUND SPICES ARE FINE

Ground spices are fine but only if they're fairly fresh. If you're planning to use some dusty old spice that has been festering at the back of the cupboard, don't expect it to taste of anything. If you're buying freshly ground spices, buy the best you can afford and change them regularly. Whole spices last longer because their oils are kept intact, but you'll need to invest in some time in the form of a pestle and mortar, or money in the form of an electric spice grinder.

09
EAT WITH YOUR HANDS

Everything tastes better when eaten with your hands (with the exception of soup). 'Why would you want to taste the metal of a fork first?' my mum asked me. Good question, Mum.

10
SHARE YOUR FOOD

There's no greater joy than to eat around a crowded table with friends and family at home.

STARTERS + SNACKS

No Indian mother ever taught her child not to snack between meals.

In India, snacking is not a dirty word. This probably has something to do with the fact that snacks are predominantly freshly made by real people right in front of you. In England, most snacks tend to be processed. Packets of things made by machines, with ingredients called E107 rather than 'chickpeas'.

That's not to say the other sort of snacks aren't available in India. Big companies and high street chains selling processed and fast food have moved into Indian cities, trying to tempt Indians away from the streets and into shopping malls. However, by and large, Indians from bankers to street kids are wobbling their heads at this sort of stuff, and the man on the street still reigns supreme, with his upturned fuel can, selling his freshly made snacks with his dubious health-and-safety credentials.

He is often just one man, with one pan and one dish. His stall won't have a name or be listed; he will be known by a name such as 'the pav bhaji wallah at Tolly roundabout' or 'the egg bhurji man on Churchgate opposite the school'. But he may have had his patch for the last thirty years, serving the same thing, like his father before him and possibly even his father before him. And you can taste every single day of those thirty years that have made the dish you order a thing of utter perfection.

My favourite snacks are the ones that pack an almighty punch and leave you feeling like you need to sit down. They are the ones I love to make for myself, my family and hard-core Indian-snack enthusiasts. They will take you on a roller coaster of flavours, tastes and textures from first bite to last; majestic snacks like blackened sweetcorn chaat (see page 26) or new potato and chickpea chaat (page 37). Then there are those snacks which everyone loves and are irritatingly addictive: beetroot shami kebabs (page 25) and Darjeeling momos (page 41). There is the cheela (page 42), the ultimate fallback, the gold champion of a snack, a pancake into which you can throw anything, made with every Indian's favourite store-cupboard ingredient, chickpea flour. And finally, there are those snacks that I would eat a lot more of, if only they weren't deep-fried. I can't contemplate a life without poppadoms, samosas or onion bhajis, so I have created some recipes (pages 21, 34 and 28) where you don't have to deep-fry.

You might be wondering why I've been talking about snacks all this time and haven't once mentioned starters. This is because starters don't exist in Indian home cooking. You can, however, use every one of the recipes in this chapter as a starter.

HOME-MADE POPPADOMS
WITH TOMATO MASALA

(masala papad)

I love a tower of restaurant poppadoms and a parade of chutneys as much as the next woman, but they can be overly greasy and salty. These poppadoms are neither, and you can make them at home in huge, family-sized rounds. Or, if you're not into sharing, you can make lots of small, canapé-sized rounds using a cookie cutter. These are made with chickpea flour because I prefer the flavour, so don't be surprised if these end up a little thicker than the ones you're used to.

Makes **4 big sharing poppadoms**
   (enough for 8 or more)

FOR THE TOMATO MASALA
500g ripe tomatoes
½ a red onion
1½ green finger chillies
15g fresh coriander
1 teaspoon salt
3 tablespoons lime juice

FOR THE POPPADOMS
250g chickpea (gram) flour
   (plus extra to dust)
2 teaspoons nigella seeds
¾ teaspoon ground black pepper
¾ teaspoon salt
1 teaspoon ground cumin
½ teaspoon chilli powder
3 tablespoons rapeseed oil

Chop the tomatoes very finely, then do the same with the red onion, green chillies and coriander. Place in a serving bowl with the salt and lime juice, stir to mix, and refrigerate until needed. (The longer it sits, the tastier it will be.)

To make the poppadoms, preheat the oven to 160°C/320°F/gas 3 and line a couple of baking trays with lightly oiled foil. Place the chickpea flour in a large mixing bowl, and add the nigella seeds, black pepper, salt, cumin and chilli powder. Mix thoroughly, then add the oil and work through with your fingers until the mixture resembles breadcrumbs.

Make a well in the middle of the mix. Little by little, add 100ml of water, mixing as you go – you may not need it all. Knead the dough until it comes together into a ball; it will be slightly tacky to the touch. Remove the dough from the bowl, wrap tightly in cling film and leave to rest for 30 minutes.

Lightly flour a clean surface and split the dough into 4 balls (about 100g each). Take the first ball, flatten between your palms and coat both sides in flour. Roll it into as big a round as you can, 25cm in diameter if possible, adding a little more flour if it starts to stick. It's not easy to get poppadoms round, but if you don't manage it, they will look rustic (to use estate agent terms).

When rolled, place on the oiled tray and repeat. You may need to cook them in a couple of batches, in which case cover the dough and roll it out just before baking, so it doesn't dry out. Bake in the oven for 20 minutes, or until they are golden brown and hard when you tap them.

To serve, place the poppadoms on large plates and use a slotted spoon to spoon over the tomato masala, leaving the liquid behind. Or serve the masala in a bowl next to the poppadoms.

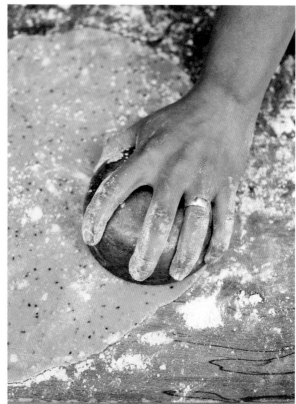

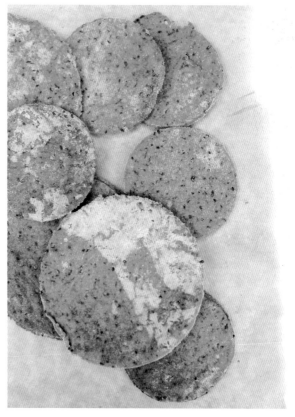

BEETROOT SHAMI KEBABS

(chukandar ke kebab)

Deep in the midst of Lucknow Chowk, beyond the donkey carts and men with their piles of saffron naans, is Tunday Kebabs. It serves one of India's most prized kebabs, the stuff of legend. The story goes that it was created by a one-armed man, Haj Murad Ali, for a toothless Mughal ruler over 100 years ago to melt in the mouth and relieve the king of any awkward public dining situations. Although this isn't a recipe for that actual kebab, it is my recipe for the closest vegetarian version.

These kebabs are delicate, with a crisp charcoal exterior and a marshmallow-soft centre, so be gentle while you're making them. Lovely with hot naan bread (see page 220), a salad like my leaves, herbs and curds (page 140), and cucumber and mint raita (page 247).

Makes **18** | Serves **6**

550g raw beetroot
225g soft paneer, like Savera or
   home-made (see page 286)
2 tablespoons lemon juice
4cm ginger, peeled and grated
3 cloves of garlic, crushed
2 green finger chillies,
   finely chopped
1 teaspoon garam masala
1½ teaspoons salt
4 tablespoons chickpea
   (gram) flour
30g fresh coriander,
   finely sliced
1 medium egg
rapeseed oil

Top and tail the beetroot, place in a pan of cold water on a medium heat, bring to the boil and cook until tender and a knife slides easily through them. Depending on their size, this could take from 40 minutes to 1 hour. Drain and leave to cool, then slip the skins off using your fingers or the back of a knife (wear rubber gloves if you don't fancy having pink hands for the rest of the day). Mash the beets as finely as you can.

Pop the beetroot mash into a frying pan over a medium heat and stir-fry for around 5 minutes. Crumble the paneer into the beetroot, add the lemon juice, ginger, garlic, green chillies, garam masala and salt, and stir for another couple of minutes. Take the pan off the heat, add the chickpea flour and coriander, and mix really well. Leave the mixture to cool down, then add the egg and mix thoroughly.

Lay a sheet of greaseproof paper or foil on a flat surface. Take an egg-sized bit of mixture, roll into a ball, then flatten it into a patty around 6cm in diameter. Place on the foil and repeat with the rest of the mixture to make 18 kebabs in total.

Put a teaspoon of oil into a non-stick frying pan on a high heat. When hot, add 4 kebabs and fry for around 1½ minutes on one side. Turn and fry for another 1½ minutes, or until crispy. Repeat with the rest, then transfer to a serving plate with some cucumber and mint raita and hot naan bread.

BLACKENED SWEETCORN CHAAT

(makai ki chaat)

This is just the sort of thing I love to eat when I'm at a low ebb mid-afternoon, as its lip-smacking flavours jolt the senses, seduce the taste buds and make you want to punch your fist in the air for being alive. The key here is getting the right levels of chilli, lemon and salt – I like mine on the upper edge of what's acceptable. Start slow and keep on adding, tasting and adjusting each ingredient until it's perfect for you. This is good by itself, but you can also serve it with hot chapattis (see page 288).

Serves **4**

4 corn cobs, or 2 x 340g
   tins of sweetcorn, drained
2 teaspoons cumin
   seeds, crushed
25g unsalted butter
¾ teaspoon ground
   black pepper
½ teaspoon chilli powder
   (plus extra to serve)
just over ½ teaspoon salt
2½ tablespoons fresh
   lemon juice
½ a red onion, finely diced
20g fresh coriander,
   finely chopped
a handful of sev
   (chickpea noodles)
1 lemon, quartered, to serve

If you're using fresh corn, pull off the husks and any loose silky threads. Bring a pan of water to the boil and carefully lower in the cobs. Boil for around 8 minutes, until tender. Drain, then wash under cold water. To slice off the kernels, make sure the cob sits flat (slice off the stem on the bottom of the cob if not) and place in a shallow dish. Hold the pointy end firmly with one hand and, with the other, slice close to the core, letting the blade move down the cob.

Set a large frying pan over a medium heat and, when hot, put the cumin into it. Stir-fry for a minute, until you can smell it, then add the butter and let it melt. Turn the heat up and, when the pan starts to smoke, add the corn. Cook for 6 to 8 minutes – don't stir too frequently, so it has a chance to blacken and caramelize, but watch out as the odd kernel may pop. When the corn has a good amount of colour, add the black pepper, chilli powder, salt and lemon juice and let it sizzle off.

Divide the corn between four plates and scatter over the red onion, coriander and sev. Sprinkle a little chilli powder over the top and place a wedge of lemon on the side.

GF

BAKED ONION BHAJIS

(pyaz ke pakore)

These are a step forward from the deep-fried favourites: they are healthier, more pleasant to cook, and just as tasty. I like to serve these with a fresh coriander or mango chutney, or beetroot raita (see page 248).

Makes **24**

3cm ginger, peeled and
   roughly chopped
1 green finger chilli, chopped
2 teaspoons cumin seeds
salt
1kg brown onions
4 tablespoons rapeseed oil
180g chickpea (gram) flour
40g fresh coriander,
   roughly chopped
½ teaspoon red chilli powder
1 teaspoon ground coriander
½ teaspoon ground turmeric
1 tablespoon lemon juice

Preheat the oven to 180°C/350°F/gas 4 and line two baking trays with lightly oiled foil. Put the ginger, green chilli and cumin seeds into a pestle and mortar along with a small pinch of salt, bash to a coarse paste and leave to one side.

Peel and halve the onions, then slice them into 0.5cm half-moon shapes. Put the oil into a large frying pan over a medium heat and, when hot, add the onions. Fry for around 15 minutes, stirring occasionally, until they're translucent and just soft enough to cut with a wooden spoon.

Put the onions into a bowl and add the ginger, green chilli and cumin paste, along with the chickpea flour, fresh coriander, chilli powder, ground coriander, turmeric, lemon juice and 1½ teaspoons of salt. Mix thoroughly and, little by little, add up to 30ml of water, until you have a very thick batter.

Take a tablespoon of the mixture and drop it on to a tray. Repeat with the rest of the mix, leaving a couple of centimetres between each bhaji.

Bake for 25 to 35 minutes, until the bhajis start to crisp up and brown on top. Remove from the oven – you may need to gently lever them off the foil using a palette knife – and place on a plate alongside some chutney before devouring.

CHESTNUT MUSHROOM +
WALNUT SAMOSAS

(masaruma akharōta samose)

I have given recipes for these well-loved triangles of joy in *Made in India*, but here are a couple of new variations. These can be made in advance, frozen and then baked at the last minute, making them perfect for parties. Follow the instructions on page 34 on how to fill, fold and bake your samosas.

As combinations go, mushrooms and walnuts are a mighty pair: smoky, earthy and addictive. The key to making these is to ensure the seasoning is strong (as the taste will be muted slightly by the samosa pastry) and the mixture is dry (a wet mixture will make for a soggy samosa).

NOTE: A food processor will make light work of chopping your mushrooms and grinding your walnuts.

Makes **18 to 22**

150g walnut halves
750g chestnut mushrooms,
   cleaned
3 tablespoons rapeseed oil
1 teaspoon black mustard seeds
1 teaspoon cumin seeds
½ teaspoon nigella seeds
1 large brown onion, diced
2 green finger chillies,
   finely chopped
3cm ginger, peeled and grated
6 large cloves of garlic, crushed
1¼ teaspoons salt
1 teaspoon ground black pepper

Throw the walnuts into a food processor and grind very finely, then remove and set to one side. Put the mushrooms into the food processor, chop until pea-sized and set these to one side too.

Warm the oil in your largest frying pan over a medium heat and, when hot, add the mustard, cumin and nigella seeds. When the seeds start to wriggle, add the onion and cook for around 10 minutes, until soft and starting to brown. Add the green chillies, ginger and garlic and cook for a further 5 minutes, or until the onion looks like dark jewels, then add the mushrooms. Don't worry if they come up to the brim of your pan, as they'll soon reduce.

Gently fold the ingredients together, add the salt and black pepper and cook for around 15 minutes, until the water evaporates – there should only be the tiniest trace of water in the bottom of the pan, or else you'll have soggy samosas. Add the walnuts, cook for another 3 minutes, then take off the heat and leave to cool before you make the samosas.

LEEK, PEA + MINT SAMOSAS

(hara pyaz, matar, pudina ke samose)

These hot and sweet tangled leeks work really well with peas and mint to make an elegant and light samosa. Best served in the summer with a glass of crisp white wine. Follow the instructions on page 34 on how to fill, fold and bake your samosas.

Makes **18 to 22**

750g trimmed leeks
2 tablespoons rapeseed oil
1 tablespoon unsalted butter
1 teaspoon black mustard seeds
2 red onions, finely sliced
4cm ginger, peeled and grated
200g peas (fresh or defrosted)
1½ teaspoons garam masala
¾ teaspoon ground cumin
¾ teaspoon chilli powder
½ teaspoon ground turmeric
1¼ teaspoons salt
1 tablespoon lemon juice
10g fresh mint leaves

Wash the leeks well, remove any papery outer layers, then slice into 0.5cm rounds and leave to one side. Heat the oil and butter in a large frying pan and, when hot, add the mustard seeds. When they pop, add the onion and fry for around 10 minutes, until soft and golden, stirring occasionally. Add the ginger, stir-fry for a minute, then add the leeks.

Cook for a further 10 minutes until soft and sweet, then add the peas, garam masala, cumin, chilli powder, turmeric, salt and lemon juice. Mix thoroughly, cook for a couple more minutes, then take off the heat and allow to cool. When cooled a little – just before making the samosas – chop the mint leaves, add to the mix and stir well.

HOW TO MAKE SAMOSAS

Makes **18 to 22**

1–1¼ x 270g packs of filo
    pastry (each pack makes
    18 samosas)
100g unsalted butter, melted
optional: nigella or cumin
    seeds, to decorate

Preheat the oven to 200°C/400°F/gas 6 and line two baking trays with baking paper.

Delicately unroll one sheet of pastry and place on a large chopping board. Brush it lightly with melted butter and layer with another sheet of pastry. Cut the sheets into three horizontal strips (around 10 x 25cm), using a sharp knife.

Make a cone shape at one side of the strip, place 1 heaped tablespoon of the filling inside the cone, then fold the open side of the cone into the rest of the filo strip to cover and seal it. Keep folding over the rest of the pastry around the shape of the cone until you come to the end of the strip. Cut off any excess pastry and stick the strip down with a brush of melted butter. Pop the samosa on a tray and repeat.

To bake your samosas, brush them on both sides with butter, sprinkle with the nigella or cumin seeds if using, and bake for 15 minutes, or until golden and crispy. Serve with cucumber and mint raita (see page 247) or some mango chutney.

NOTE: If you don't want to bake your samosas straight away, put them in a single layer on a non-stick tray without brushing with butter, then place in the freezer. (You can put them into bags when they're properly frozen.) To cook from frozen, place in a single layer on a lined baking tray and bake for 20 to 25 minutes, until golden, brushing with melted butter halfway through.

NEW POTATO + CHICKPEA CHAAT

(aloo chana chaat)

The flavours in this incredibly popular Indian street-side snack will dance in your mouth. Buttery potatoes wrap around the chickpeas in an open embrace. They're followed by a flourish of shallots, a smouldering slick of date and tamarind chutney and the crunch of sev. Beats a packet of crisps any day. Although tamarind and sev (chickpea noodles) might seem hard to find, they are nearly always available in the Asian section of big supermarkets. Look for thin or 'nylon' sev – but if you can't find any, a little Bombay mix works a treat.

NOTE: As tamarind paste varies from brand to brand, add it gradually until it tastes good to you.

Serves 4

75g dates, pitted
3 teaspoons tamarind paste
salt
2 tablespoons Greek yoghurt
600g baby new potatoes
25g unsalted butter
1 teaspoon cumin seeds,
    roughly ground
⅓ teaspoon ground
    black pepper
1 teaspoon ground ginger
1 green finger chilli,
    finely chopped
1 x 400g tin of chickpeas,
    drained
1 large banana shallot,
    finely diced
juice of 1 lemon
20g fresh coriander,
    finely chopped
a handful of thin sev
    (chickpea noodles)

Prepare the date and tamarind chutney first. Blend the dates together with the tamarind paste, a pinch of salt and 100ml of water, then leave to one side.

Mix the yoghurt with a couple of tablespoons of water until you can drizzle it using a spoon, then leave to one side.

Wash and boil the potatoes for around 15 minutes, until tender and a knife can slip through them easily. Drain, tip on to a plate and crush slightly with a fork or the bottom of a sturdy cup.

Put the butter into a wide-bottomed frying pan over a medium heat. When melted, add the ground cumin seeds, black pepper, ginger, green chilli and ¾ teaspoon of salt. Stir, then add the potatoes. Leave the potatoes to crisp and char for around 5 minutes, then throw in the chickpeas, shallot and lemon juice. Leave to heat through for a few minutes. Add a couple of tablespoons of date and tamarind chutney, stir to mix and take off the heat.

To serve, divide the mixture between four shallow bowls, spoon over the yoghurt, dot over the remaining chutney, and top with the fresh coriander and sev.

GF

THE QUEEN'S BOMBAY NUTS

(rani ke chevda)

According to the *Daily Telegraph*, in 2013 Buckingham Palace had a major issue on its hands. Mysteriously the Queen's Bombay mix was slowly disappearing. Disgruntled, our glorious leader decided to take matters into her own hands and keep a closer eye on her snacks.

Ma'am, this recipe is dedicated to you. Please treat it as a back-up when you notice your supplies are reaching perilously low levels.

Makes 500g

500g unsalted mixed nuts
    (e.g. cashews, walnuts,
    pecans, almonds, pistachios)
3 tablespoons rapeseed oil
1½ teaspoons salt
2 teaspoons chilli powder
2 teaspoons garam masala
1 teaspoon sugar
¾ teaspoon ground turmeric
2 tablespoons chickpea
    (gram) flour

Preheat the oven to 150°C/300°F/gas 2 and line two baking trays with foil or baking paper.

Place the nuts in a large mixing bowl, add the oil and mix so that the nuts are well coated. Put the rest of the ingredients into another bowl and mix together. Then add the dry ingredients to the nuts and combine thoroughly.

Spread the nuts out over the two trays and bake for 30 minutes, shuffling the nuts halfway through to make sure they cook evenly.

Take the nuts out of the oven and leave to cool. One can eat them all by one's royal self, share with the rest of the household or, when completely cool, put in some Tupperware to eat within a few weeks.

(GF) (DF) (VE)

DARJEELING MOMOS
WITH CHILLI SAUCE

These fun little dumplings are the most popular street snack in Darjeeling, thanks to the thousands of Tibetans who have made the town their home since the 1960s. They're enjoyable to make, but more so on a weekend when you're over-indexing on enthusiasm and patience. If you're running short on either, you can buy momo wrappers from a Chinese supermarket, or roll out a sheet of dough and use a cookie cutter to cut the wrappers out. The method below is for rolling them individually.

NOTE: If you don't have a food processor to pulse the filling, just finely shred the vegetables before cooking.

Makes **20**

FOR THE MOMO WRAPPERS
200g plain flour
   (plus extra to dust)
¼ teaspoon salt

FOR THE CHILLI SAUCE
4 tablespoons dark soy sauce
1½ teaspoons chilli flakes
2 teaspoons rice or white
   wine vinegar
2 teaspoons sugar or honey

FOR THE FILLING
3 tablespoons rapeseed oil
4cm ginger, peeled and grated
3 cloves of garlic, crushed
2 medium carrots (about
   200g), peeled and
   roughly diced
⅓ of a head of green cabbage
   (200g), shredded
200g hard paneer,
   roughly diced
⅓ teaspoon salt
2 teaspoons dark soy sauce
4 spring onions, finely sliced

First make the momo wrappers. Mix the flour and salt in a big bowl, make a well and, little by little, add 110ml of water. Knead the dough until smooth, then cover with a clean, slightly damp towel.

Put the ingredients for the chilli sauce into a bowl and stir briskly to dissolve the sugar. To make the filling, put a tablespoon of oil in a large frying pan over a medium heat and, when hot, add the ginger and garlic. Stir-fry for a minute, add the carrots and fry for another couple of minutes. Add the cabbage, paneer, salt and soy sauce, and cook until the vegetables are tender. The mixture should be quite dry – if not, turn the heat up until the liquid evaporates. Add the spring onions, then take off the heat and allow to cool. Tip into a food processor and pulse until finely chopped.

Prepare a couple of lightly floured baking trays. Using your hands, roll the dough into a long even sausage shape and divide into 4 pieces. Take one and cover the rest with a damp tea towel. Cut the portion of dough into 5 pieces. Roll each piece into a ball, dust with flour and, on a well-floured surface, roll out to around 8cm in diameter. Lay the prepared wrappers on the trays and continue with the rest of the dough.

When the wrappers are rolled, take a heaped teaspoon of the filling and put it in the middle of the wrapper. Fold the wrapper in half over the filling. Press shut, then, starting from one side, fold over the corner of the seam and repeat until you reach the seam's end. Brush the momos with a little oil and lay on a non-stick surface.

Heat a tablespoon of oil in a large lidded non-stick frying pan. Place half the momos in the pan (or as many as will comfortably fit) and fry for around 3 minutes, until brown on the bottom. Turn the heat down to low, add 3 tablespoons of water and cover with the lid. Steam them for a further 4 to 5 minutes, until the liquid has evaporated and the momo wrappers are translucent, then repeat with the rest. Eat hot, dunked in the chilli sauce.

CHICKPEA PANCAKES WITH PANEER + LIME PICKLE

(paneer cheela)

Some recipes are as necessary in the kitchen as a sharp knife and the radio. This trusty, tasty pancake made with chickpea flour is one of them. You can throw almost any herb, vegetable or spice in it, but this lime pickle and paneer topping is a lip-smacking way to jazz it up. It's helpful to have a ladle so that all the batter can hit the pan in one go. As with all pancakes, the first one is always the odd one out. Which means, by rights, it goes to the chef.

Makes 4 to 6 small pancakes

150g chickpea (gram) flour
½ teaspoon ground turmeric
1 teaspoon garam masala
¼ teaspoon baking powder
salt
225g soft paneer, like Savera or
   home-made (see page 286)
1¼ tablespoons lime pickle,
   like Patak's
20g fresh coriander
10g fresh dill (plus
   extra to serve)
rapeseed oil

Put the chickpea flour into a medium-sized bowl and add the turmeric, garam masala, baking powder and ½ teaspoon of salt. Mix thoroughly, then make a well and whisk in 240ml of water. Rest the batter for 20 minutes.

While the batter is resting, chop the paneer into 1cm cubes. (If it's the fresh sort, crumble with the back of a spoon or your fingers – you'll get some tasty little crumbs that way.)

Cut the lime pickle up, so there are no big chunks of lime. Put a tablespoon of oil into a frying pan over a medium heat. When hot, add the paneer and cook for around 4 minutes, until the paneer starts to crisp up. Add the pickle, stir through, and season with ¼ teaspoon of salt. Take off the heat.

Chop the herbs, add to the batter and stir to combine. Set a small non-stick pan over a medium heat. Pour a drizzle of oil into the pan and tip from side to side to coat the bottom. Pour a ladleful of batter into the pan and cook the pancake for 1 minute, or until the edges start to brown, then flip using a fish slice. Cook for another minute, flip again, then repeat this process twice, cooking the pancake for 4 minutes in total. Remove from the pan and repeat with the rest of the batter. To keep the pancakes warm, wrap them in foil.

To serve, scatter over the paneer mixture and a little chopped dill.

GF

DHOKLA

'Eat it once, love it for ever': that would be dhokla's slogan of choice. You might not expect to find an object of desire tucked away in a fluffy steamed chickpea bread, but what started out as a humble Gujarati snack is now one of India's national treasures (and 1 billion Indians voting with their stomachs can't be wrong).

It's not difficult to make this snack, but it involves steaming, which I will guide you through. The other special ingredient you'll need is Eno fruit salt. It is completely safe to eat and available from the pharmacy aisle of supermarkets or from an Asian grocery store.

Serves 4 to 6 as a snack

1 tablespoon rapeseed oil
  (plus extra to grease)
110g chickpea (gram) flour
110ml Greek yoghurt
2 tablespoons lemon juice
1 teaspoon salt
½ a green finger chilli,
  finely sliced
2cm ginger, peeled and grated
1 teaspoon Eno fruit salt
1 teaspoon black mustard seeds
1 teaspoon sesame seeds
10 fresh curry leaves
½ tablespoon desiccated or
  fresh grated coconut
a handful of chopped coriander

First set up your steamer: either use a steamer or, if you don't have one, find a large casserole pot with a tight lid into which you can fit a sandwich cake tin. Find something to rest the cake tin on inside the pot. I use a small glass ramekin, but you could use some scrunched-up balls of foil. Pour water halfway up whatever you're resting your cake tin on, then lightly grease the cake tin and set to one side.

Put the chickpea flour into a bowl and add 110ml water, mixing it in little by little so the batter doesn't end up lumpy. Then add the yoghurt, lemon juice, salt, green chilli, ginger and the Eno fruit salt.

Bring the water in the casserole pot to a boil. Once boiling, tip the batter into the oiled cake tin and carefully lower into the pot. Steam for 8 minutes. You can check whether it's done by placing a knife into the batter. If it comes out cleanly, it's done. If not, put the lid back on for another couple of minutes. Once done, remove the cake tin and leave to cool (the dhokla will be much easier to remove).

Just before serving, make a tarka: heat the oil in a small frying pan and, when hot, add the mustard seeds, sesame seeds and curry leaves. Fry until the mustard seeds pop and the curry leaves crackle, then take off the heat and pour over the top of the dhokla.

Scatter over the coconut and fresh coriander, and serve.

PEA, DILL + MINT SOUP

(hare matar ka shorba)

A spicy and fresh pea soup packed full of fresh herbs and with a good chilli hit.

NOTE: You will need a blender for this recipe.

Serves 4

rapeseed oil
1 large brown onion,
    finely sliced
3cm ginger, peeled and grated
3 cloves of garlic, crushed
3 green finger chillies,
    finely chopped
900g frozen petit pois
600ml hot vegetable stock
juice of ½ a lemon
2 teaspoons garam masala
30g fresh mint leaves, chopped
    (plus extra to decorate)
25g fresh dill, chopped
2 teaspoons cumin seeds
a pinch of salt

Heat 2 tablespoons of oil in a deep saucepan and, when hot, add the onion. Fry until soft and translucent, but not golden, then add the ginger, garlic and green chillies. Stir for a couple of minutes, then add the peas, hot stock, lemon juice and garam masala.

Bring the peas to the boil, add the herbs, stir to mix, then take off the heat. Whizz up in a blender, pour back into the pan and reheat gently.

In the meantime, make a hot cumin-flavoured oil (tarka) to pour over the top of the soup. Pour a slug of oil into a small frying pan over a medium heat and, when hot, add the cumin seeds. Leave to sizzle until they brown, add the salt and take off the heat.

Transfer the soup into four bowls, sprinkle over the remaining mint leaves and pour over the cumin oil.

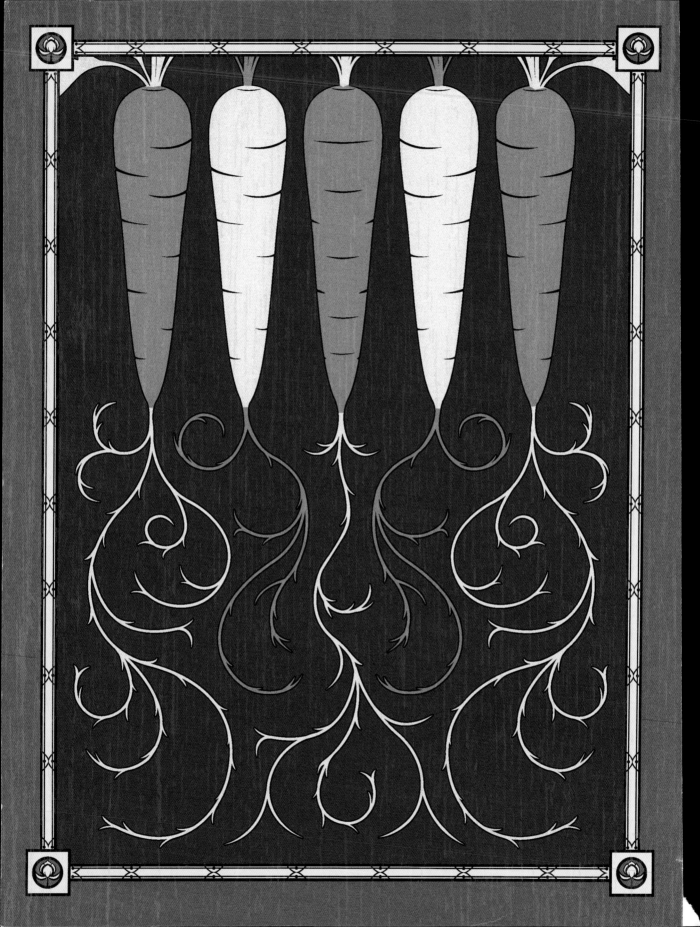

ROOTS, SQUASHES, TUBERS + OTHER THINGS

Everything grows in Lincolnshire: roots, shoots and fruit. In the fields behind my family home, there's a potato farm. To either side of our road, in a patchwork of fields, there are beetroot, maize and rapeseed, while in the distance, pink pigs light up the landscape. This is the farm of England.

Since my family arrived here in 1972, we have curried and spiced almost every root, tuber and squash within the county borders – some untraditional in Indian cuisine and introduced to us by neighbours and friends. While much produce is now available the whole year round, the seasons still give our little farming village a tempo: a change of scenery, weather, produce and appetite. In January and February, in the grip of midwinter, brassicas such as cabbages, as heavy as the layers of fog that lie across the flats of the county, are at their peak and on my table. The weather lends itself to dishes packed full of root vegetables flavoured with garam (warming) masalas containing black pepper, cinnamon, cumin and cloves.

Just when winter seems interminable, the daffodils arrive, followed by sacks upon sacks of new potatoes, the main crop in our village. Spring offers precious little else in terms of local roots, so we eat those year-round stalwarts: cauliflowers, leeks and onions.

Early summer sees soil-covered baby beetroot with large thrusting leaves lining the market stalls outside my flat. I buy big batches, boil them, then mix them with cooling yoghurt, curry leaves and coconut to make beetroot pachadi (see page 51).

In late summer, I look forward to a blaze of golden sweetcorn. I try to buy them in their husks, as they deteriorate quickly otherwise, with small juicy kernels. We eat these freshly blistered cobs messily, slathered in lemon, salt and chilli, or Gujarati-style in a deeply savoury chickpea and peanut sauce (page 76).

At the start of autumn, mushrooms gatherers bring amazing fungi to the market. I save my money for the delicate chanterelles to crown meals, but buy the chestnut mushrooms in larger quantities to spice and cook more heavy-handedly in one of India's favourite dishes, kheema (page 72).

Later in the season, there is a huge variety of different pumpkins and squashes. They are some of my favourites to cook: their sweet flesh can stand up to some robust spicing, and you can feed a whole family heartily on just a single one.

BEETROOT PACHADI

You might think that beetroot is unknown in India, but in fact it is eaten all over the country. In this Keralan beetroot and coconut dish, big delicious flavours are created very simply. For that reason, I keep coming back to this recipe time and time again. It is often served as a side dish with other meat or vegetable curries. I like to eat it with dal, or cucumber and mint raita (see page 247) and tamarind and caramelized red onion rice (page 192).

The recipe comes from an unassuming little restaurant in Kochi called Casa Linda, run by a beautiful woman with a smile so large and a heart so big that there is practically no space for anything else in the room.

NOTE: You will need a food processor or blender for this recipe.

Serves 4 as part of a
    main course

800g raw beetroot
2 teaspoons black mustard
    seeds
20 fresh curry leaves
55g desiccated or fresh
    grated coconut
4 cloves of garlic
1½ green finger chillies
3cm ginger, peeled and grated
1 teaspoon cumin seeds
300ml Greek yoghurt
2 tablespoons rapeseed oil
1 teaspoon salt

Top and tail the beetroot, place in a pan of cold water on a medium heat, bring to the boil and cook until tender and a knife slides easily through them. This could take from 40 minutes to an hour, depending on the size of your beetroot.

Meanwhile, make the coconut paste. Add half the mustard seeds, half the curry leaves, all the coconut, garlic, green chillies, ginger, cumin seeds and half the yoghurt to a food processor, and blend to a fine paste. Add the remaining yoghurt and blend again, then place in a bowl and set aside.

Once the beetroot has boiled, drain and leave to cool, then slip the skins off with your fingers or the back of a knife (wear rubber gloves if you don't fancy having pink hands for the rest of the day). Cut the beetroot in half and then into wedges, 1–2cm at the thick end.

In a large lidded frying pan, heat the oil and, once hot, add the remaining curry leaves and mustard seeds. When they start to crackle, add the beetroot, stir-fry for a couple of minutes, then add the coconut yoghurt paste and the salt. Stir to mix, pop the lid on the pan and cook for 8 minutes, then take off the heat and serve.

SHREDDED ROTI WITH RED CABBAGE + CARROT

(kottu roti)

This dish is a tasty jumbled heap of shredded bread, crispy vegetables and egg, seasoned with a fiery mix of spices. It's a perfect way to use up old rotis and any veg that might have overstayed its welcome in the bottom of the fridge.

Part roadside spectacle, part musical entertainment, in Sri Lanka the chefs use huge, noisy metal blades to rhythmically chop and mix everything until it comes together in one democratic and harmonious ensemble. You don't need a metallic orchestra for this recipe, however: a frying pan, sharp knife and some enthusiasm will do.

NOTE: You will need a blender for this recipe.

Serves 2 as a main course

200g tinned or fresh
   plum tomatoes
4 cloves of garlic
4cm ginger, peeled
1½ green finger chillies
2 tablespoons rapeseed oil
1 red onion, sliced
1 teaspoon cumin
   seeds, crushed
2 tablespoons soy sauce
½ a red cabbage (300g),
   finely shredded
2 large carrots (about
   300g), peeled and
   cut into matchsticks
3 flatbreads or paratha,
   shredded into 1cm ribbons
2 eggs, lightly beaten
1 teaspoon salt
4 spring onions, finely sliced
a handful of fresh
   coriander, chopped

Put the tomatoes, garlic, ginger and green chillies into a blender and pulse to a paste.

Warm the oil in a frying pan over a medium heat and, when hot, add the red onion. Cook for 10 minutes, or until golden and soft, then add the blended tomato paste. Cook for around 5 minutes, then add the cumin seeds and soy sauce. Stir to mix, and add the cabbage and carrots.

Cook for 6 minutes, or until the cabbage and carrots soften but still have a good crunch, then add the shredded flatbreads. Fold into the pan using a wooden spoon and cook for 4 minutes, then add the eggs and salt. Toss the mixture for a couple of minutes, until the egg is cooked, then take off the heat.

Transfer to a serving plate or divide between dinner plates, and sprinkle the spring onions and coriander over the top.

SWEET POTATO VINDALOO

In England, the vindaloo is an ear-tinglingly hot curry, but it wasn't always that way. It started life as *vinho e alhos*, a popular Portuguese dish that made its way over to Goa with Portuguese explorers in the 1500s. Traditionally a wine and garlic stew, it was transformed into the modern-day dish using white wine vinegar and garlic, combined with a warming garam masala of pepper, cloves and cinnamon.

In this recipe, the sweet potato works really well with the spices and tomato to make a sweet, sour and pungent curry. And yes, it's hot, but not mind-blowingly so.

Serves 4 as a main course

4 tablespoons rapeseed oil
6 cloves
1 star anise
20 black peppercorns
8cm cinnamon stick
2 teaspoons cumin seeds
6 cloves of garlic, crushed
4cm ginger, peeled and grated
  (plus extra to serve)
5 tablespoons white
  wine vinegar
¾ level tablespoon chilli powder
  (or to taste)
2 medium onions, finely sliced
1 teaspoon salt
1 teaspoon sugar
1 x 400g tin of plum tomatoes
1kg sweet potatoes, peeled and
  chopped into 3cm chunks
yoghurt, to serve

Put 1 tablespoon of the oil into a large lidded frying pan over a medium heat and, when hot, add the cloves, star anise, black peppercorns, cinnamon stick and cumin seeds. Stir-fry for around 2 minutes, until the peppercorns and cloves swell and you can smell all the spices, then take off the heat.

Tip the spices into a spice grinder or pestle and mortar and grind them up. Add the garlic, ginger and vinegar, grind some more until you have a smooth paste, then mix in the chilli powder.

Put the remaining oil into the same pan over a medium heat and, when hot, add the onions. Cook for 15 minutes, or until brown and caramelized, stirring occasionally, then add the spice paste, salt and sugar. Cook for a couple of minutes, then add the plum tomatoes, tipping them out of the tin with one hand while crushing them with the other. Fill the tomato tin half full with water and tip into the pan. Put the lid on the pan and cook for around 5 minutes, then add the sweet potatoes.

Bring the curry to a boil, reduce to a simmer and cover with the lid again. Cook for 20 to 25 minutes, until the sweet potato is completely tender, stirring occasionally. Serve with dollops of yoghurt and hot basmati rice.

ROASTED ROOT VEGETABLE MADRAS

You don't have to use baby vegetables for this dish. I use them because they're sweet and beautiful, but you could use larger roots and cut them down to size.

Serves 4

1.2kg mix of baby carrots,
    parsnips, turnips
    and potatoes
rapeseed oil
2 teaspoons ground cumin
salt and ground black pepper
10 fresh curry leaves
1 large red onion,
    finely chopped
4 cloves of garlic, crushed
3cm ginger, peeled and grated
2 green finger chillies,
    finely sliced
1 x 400g tin of plum tomatoes
½ tablespoon tomato puree
1 teaspoon garam masala
⅓ teaspoon ground turmeric
1 teaspoon honey

Preheat the oven to 180°C/350°F/gas 4.

Trim, wash and scrub the baby vegetables and put them on one or two large baking trays. Drizzle with oil, add 1 teaspoon of cumin and season with salt and black pepper, then mix until evenly coated. Roast for 30 to 40 minutes, until caramelized and crisp on the outside and soft inside.

In the meantime, make the Madras sauce. Put 2 tablespoons of oil into a large frying pan over a medium heat and, when hot, add the curry leaves. Let them crackle and pop for a minute, then add the onion. Cook the onion for 10 minutes, until soft and golden, then add the garlic, ginger and green chillies. Stir-fry for 3 to 4 minutes until cooked through.

Add the tomatoes and their juice to the pan, breaking them up with the back of a wooden spoon or a fork. Fill the tomato tin three-quarters full with water and add with the tomato puree, stirring to mix. Leave to cook for around 10 minutes, stir, and cook for another 5 minutes until rich and reduced. Then add the remaining teaspoon of cumin, the garam masala, turmeric and honey. Add a little water to loosen the sauce and season with salt.

To serve, add almost all the roasted baby vegetables to the sauce, leaving a few aside. Transfer to a serving dish, lay the remaining vegetables on top and serve with steamed rice or buttered chapattis (see page 288).

PUNJABI POTATO CURRY

(punjabi dum aloo)

Every state in India has its own potato curry. We Gujaratis have our own 'batata nu shaak', but I'll happily move it to one side to make room for a plate of Punjabi 'dum aloo'. In this dish, baby new potatoes are fried until they colour, then mixed with a happy congregation of cashews, onions and tomatoes. This is comfort food that never gets dull.

NOTE: You will need a blender for this recipe.

Serves **4 as a side**

80g unsalted cashews
1 teaspoon fennel seeds
1kg baby new potatoes
4 tablespoons rapeseed oil
1 large brown onion, sliced
4 cloves of garlic, crushed
3cm ginger, peeled and grated
1 x 400g tin of plum tomatoes
1 teaspoon garam masala
1 teaspoon chilli powder
1 teaspoon salt

Soak the cashews in 100ml of boiling water for 10 minutes. Meanwhile, crush the fennel seeds as finely as you can with a pestle and mortar.

Wash the potatoes if need be. Keep the smallest ones whole, but halve or quarter any of the larger ones so that they are all the same size. Heat 2 tablespoons of the oil in a lidded frying pan and fry the potatoes for around 8 minutes, until they brown a bit, stirring every now and again. Remove the potatoes to a plate.

Transfer the cashews along with their soaking liquid to a blender and pulse to a fine paste.

Put the rest of the oil into the frying pan over a medium heat and, when hot, fry the onion for 10 minutes, or until soft and golden. Add the garlic and ginger, and cook for 2 minutes, then add the tomatoes. Cook for around 5 to 8 minutes, until the sauce thickens and reduces, then add the crushed fennel seeds, garam masala, chilli powder and salt. Stir to mix, and add the cashew paste. Cook for a couple of minutes, then add around 300ml of water and stir.

Put the potatoes back into the pan, cover with the lid, and cook on a low heat for a further 10 to 15 minutes, until really tender the whole way through. You can check by sliding a knife through: if there's no resistance, they're done.

Eat with parathas (see page 218), rice, moong dal (page 170) and pickles.

SMASHED JERUSALEM ARTICHOKES WITH BUTTER, PEPPER + GARLIC

I wrote this recipe at the same time as writing my wedding invites and accidentally burned the artichokes at the bottom of the pan. It tasted so delicious with the charred, crispy bits nestled in among the buttery soft ones that I rewrote the recipe to give the artichokes a chance to crisp up a little. These are great just on toast, or as a partner to aubergine and pea curry (see page 118).

Serves 4 to 6 as a side

800g Jerusalem artichokes
50g butter or ghee
1½ teaspoons cumin seeds,
    roughly ground
4 cloves of garlic, crushed
2cm ginger, peeled and
    finely grated
1–2 green finger chillies,
    finely sliced
1 teaspoon salt
¾ teaspoon ground
    black pepper
juice of ½ a lemon
coriander stems from a 30g
    bunch, very finely chopped

Peel the Jerusalem artichokes and cut them into chunks. Throw them into a pan of cold water, bring to a boil and simmer for around 15 minutes, until the artichokes are tender and don't resist the tip of a knife. Drain and very lightly smash with a fork.

In a frying pan, heat the butter or ghee. When hot, add the cumin seeds, stir, then add the garlic, ginger, green chilli, salt and black pepper, and mix well. Put the artichokes back into the mixture, stir to mix and leave to cook for 5 minutes. Stir again, then cook for a further 5 to 10 minutes, until the artichokes start to crisp up and brown a little.

Squeeze over the lemon juice and gently toss through the coriander stems. Taste and add more salt if needed, then serve.

BUTTERNUT SQUASH
SEEKH KEBABS

These are lovely sweet and smoky squash lollipops. Don't worry if they brown or blacken while cooking: this is where the good flavours lurk. These are great served in chapattis (see page 288) with salad, and cucumber and mint raita (page 247). To make proper seekh kebabs you'll need either wooden or metal skewers.

Makes 8 skewers

1 medium butternut
   squash (600g)
rapeseed oil
1 x 400g tin of
   chickpeas, drained
4cm ginger, peeled
3 cloves of garlic
2 green finger chillies
75g breadcrumbs
15g fresh coriander,
   roughly chopped
2 teaspoons garam masala
1½ teaspoons salt
1 teaspoon ground cumin
½ teaspoon ground
   black pepper
butter

Preheat the oven to 180°C/350°F/gas 4 and line a baking tray with foil.

Peel the squash, halve it, and scoop the seeds out using a spoon. Cut the flesh into 4cm chunks. Coat with a tablespoon of oil and roast in the oven for 35 to 45 minutes until soft, then remove from the oven to cool.

Pulse the cooled squash in a food processor along with the remaining ingredients except the butter. If you don't have a food processor, mash the chickpeas and butternut together, mince the ginger, garlic and chillies, and stir in the other ingredients.

Separate the mixture into 8 balls. Roll one between your palms, then shape the mixture around the skewer to make a kebab around 10cm long. Repeat with the rest of the mixture.

To cook, heat a small knob of butter and a teaspoon of oil in the frying pan. When it starts to foam, put 4 skewers into the pan (or as many as will fit). Cook for 3 to 4 minutes, until lovely and brown, turning every minute or so. Cook the rest and serve.

GOAN BUTTERNUT SQUASH CAFREAL

Cafreal is an enchanting Goan Portuguese dish traditionally made by cooking chicken in a tangy marinade of fresh coriander, garlic, green chillies and spices. I've replaced the chicken with roasted squash, which works well with cafreal's fierce little kick. The sauce can be blended and cooked in minutes while the squash roasts, making this a great fuss-free recipe and unsung hero of midweek dinners.

NOTE: You will need a blender for this recipe.

Serves 4 as main course

1 large butternut squash (1.5kg)
rapeseed oil
1 large brown onion,
  thinly sliced
150g fresh coriander
4cm ginger, peeled
8 cloves of garlic
2 green finger chillies
1½ teaspoons ground cumin
½ teaspoon ground cinnamon
juice of ½ a lemon
1¼ teaspoons salt
½ teaspoon ground
  black pepper
1 x 400ml tin of coconut milk

Preheat the oven to 180°C/350°F/gas 4 and line two baking trays with foil.

Peel the squash, halve it, and scoop the seeds out using a spoon. Chop the flesh into 1cm-thick half-moons. Throw them into the trays and drizzle over a couple of tablespoons of oil. Mix with your hands to make sure the squash is evenly coated, then roast for 35 to 45 minutes, or until completely tender and starting to caramelize, turning halfway.

Meanwhile, make the fried onion to top the cafreal. Put a couple of tablespoons of oil into a pan over a medium heat and, when hot, add the onion. Fry for 15 to 20 minutes, until caramelized and crisp, then remove from the heat.

To make the cafreal sauce, chop the coriander, ginger, garlic and chillies, and put them into a blender. Add the cumin, cinnamon, lemon juice, salt, black pepper and coconut milk, and whizz until everything is well combined.

Place a deep saucepan over a medium heat and pour in the coriander and coconut milk mixture. Cook gently for 5 minutes, stirring occasionally. Add the roasted squash to the sauce and cook for a further 5 minutes.

Transfer to a serving dish, scatter over the fried onion and serve alongside rice.

CAULIFLOWER KORMA
WITH BLACKENED RAISINS

(gobhi korma)

This is a really great dish to make when people come round, as it's a crowd-pleaser and easy to cook. Normally, the sauce comes together at the same time as the roasted cauliflower, leaving you more time to tell your best jokes or play the spoons to your guests. A lot of the flavour in this dish comes from both caramelizing the onions and roasting the cauliflower, so don't compromise on either of those.

Serves 4 as a main course
or 6 as a side

2 large cauliflowers
   (about 1.6kg in total)
rapeseed oil
salt
2 large brown onions,
   thinly sliced
6 cloves of garlic
6cm ginger, peeled
¾ teaspoon ground cardamom
   (or finely ground seeds
   from 8 pods)
1 teaspoon ground black pepper
2 teaspoons garam masala
½ teaspoon chilli powder
100g ground almonds
2 tablespoons runny honey
500ml Greek yoghurt
200–300ml milk
a handful of raisins
a handful of flaked almonds

Heat the oven to 180°C/350°F/gas 4 and line two large baking trays with foil.

Break the cauliflower into bite-sized florets and put into a large bowl. Pour over 4 tablespoons of oil (or enough to coat them properly), then scatter over 1 teaspoon of salt. Mix with your hands until they're completely coated, and place in a single layer on the baking trays. Roast for 30 to 40 minutes, until tender and nicely browned in places. Check every 10 minutes – if the florets start to burn, cover them loosely with foil.

In the meantime, put 3 tablespoons of oil into a large frying pan over a medium heat and, when hot, add the onions. Cook for 12 to 15 minutes, until soft and browning, then crush in the garlic and grate in the ginger. Fry for a couple of minutes, then add the ground cardamom, black pepper, garam masala, chilli powder, ground almonds, honey and 1¼ teaspoons of salt (or to taste). Stir-fry for 3 minutes, then add the yoghurt.

Turn the heat down to low and cook for around 10 minutes, until the sauce starts to turn a rich gold. When the cauliflower is tender, tip it into the sauce and stir to coat. Thin the sauce to the consistency of pouring yoghurt with milk, and heat through. Check for seasoning, as you may need to add a little more salt.

Finally, put a small frying pan over a medium heat and, when hot, add the raisins and flaked almonds. Stir-fry until the raisins start to blacken and puff up and the almonds turn golden brown, then take off the heat.

To serve, scatter the raisins and toasted almonds over the top of the cauliflower, and serve with rice or chapattis (see page 288).

GF

WHOLE ROASTED CAULIFLOWER MUSSALAM

(gobhi mussalam)

This dish comes from the royal court kitchens of Uttar Pradesh, where it was a favourite of state banquets, high society and Mughal emperors. At that time, food wasn't just food, it was a way of showing off. It is still a great dinner-party dish: a head-turner at the table and great fun for your guests to pull apart slowly. This dish goes well with court jesters and goblets of wine.

NOTE: Kasoori methi are dried fenugreek leaves, which add an earthy tanginess to rich tomato sauces like this one. If you can't find them, leave them out.

Serves **4** as a main course

1 very large or 2 medium
   heads of cauliflower
   (about 1.2kg in total)
rapeseed oil
salt and ground black pepper
60g unsalted butter
2 large onions, finely chopped
4cm ginger, peeled and grated
6 cloves of garlic, crushed
2 x 400g tins of
   plum tomatoes
40g ground almonds
½ teaspoon ground cinnamon
1 tablespoon kasoori methi
¼ teaspoon ground cloves
1 teaspoon chilli powder
a handful of flaked almonds
a handful of fresh
   coriander leaves

Preheat the oven to 180°C/350°F/gas 4. Remove the leaves from the cauliflower and slice off a little of the bottom so that it sits flat. Rub the cauliflower with oil, getting inside all the nooks and crannies, and season with salt and black pepper. Place in a lidded ovenproof casserole dish, cover, and bake for 45 minutes.

Meanwhile, melt the butter in a frying pan over a medium heat. When it's bubbling, add the onions and cook for around 10 minutes, until soft and golden. Add the ginger and garlic, and cook for a couple of minutes. Add the tomatoes by pouring them in with one hand and crushing them with the other, then fill a can three-quarters full with water and pour that in too. Cook for 5 minutes, then add the ground almonds, cinnamon, kasoori methi, cloves, chilli powder and 1 teaspoon of salt. Cook for a further 5 minutes, then take off the heat.

After 45 minutes, test the cauliflower by sticking a skewer or sharp knife all the way through. It should be almost cooked, but not tender. (If it's still very firm, put it back into the oven for 10 to 15 minutes.) Pour the sauce over the cauliflower and return to the oven, uncovered, for a further 20 minutes. Toast the almond flakes for a couple of minutes in a small frying pan over a medium heat until they are light gold, then put to one side.

Check that the cauliflower is completely cooked through by pushing a skewer down the centre: it should go in with little resistance. When tender, remove from the oven, taste the sauce for salt and chilli and adjust if need be. Scatter the flaked almonds and coriander over the top, and serve with rice, dal, and a salad of your choice.

GF

PICKLED CAULIFLOWER
WITH GINGER + LIME

(achari gobhi)

Achari means 'pickled'. As with most pickled foods, this cauliflower dish helps to sharpen the edges of other, more comforting dishes at the table. It's lip-smackingly delicious, and the flavour will improve over time, so it's a good thing to make in advance. It works well with buttery flavours, like the moong dal with a garlic and cumin tarka on page 170, or the sticky mango paneer skewers on page 158, with some parathas (see page 218) thrown into the mix.

Serves 4 as part of a
   main course

2 tablespoons rapeseed oil
1 teaspoon black mustard seeds
12 fresh curry leaves
1 large cauliflower (about
   800g), broken into
   bite-sized florets
6cm of ginger, peeled
1½ green finger chillies,
   finely chopped
juice of 2 limes
1⅓ teaspoons salt
⅓ teaspoon ground turmeric
1 teaspoon ground coriander
1 teaspoon ground cumin

Put the oil into a large lidded frying pan over a medium heat and, when hot, add the mustard seeds and curry leaves. Wait for the seeds to crackle and pop, and the curry leaves to crisp up and go translucent, then add the cauliflower.

Fry the cauliflower for 5 minutes, stirring occasionally. Grate the ginger, then squeeze the juice into the pan with your hands or through a fine sieve or muslin cloth, and discard the pulp. Add the green chillies and continue to pan-fry for another 5 minutes. The cauliflower will start to char and caramelize (which is where lots of lovely flavour will come from).

When it has coloured nicely, add 4 tablespoons of water, stir through, then cover and leave to steam for 5 minutes, or until tender. Add the lime juice, salt, turmeric, ground coriander and cumin, and stir-fry for another 6 to 8 minutes, until all the liquid has evaporated.

Check the cauliflower for salt and lime – both should be well balanced – and either serve hot immediately or leave to cool and store in a container in the fridge to eat later.

MUSHROOM AND PEA KHEEMA

(masaruma matar ka keema)

My father lives just on the edge of what we consider to be normal. He prefers icing sugar in his tea, has the buttons of his back pockets removed (for fear of damaging his car upholstery), and keeps a logbook of when he waters the plants. One time, he accidentally spread mushroom compost over the lawn and we ate mushrooms in every conceivable way for months. If you find yourself in a similar situation, this is a satisfying and delicious way to make use of them.

NOTE: A food processor will make chopping a kilo of mushrooms a more feasible thing to do.

Serves **4 as a main course**

1kg chestnut mushrooms
2 tablespoons unsalted butter
1 tablespoon oil
1 teaspoon cumin seeds,
   crushed
2 red onions, finely diced
5 cloves of garlic, crushed
3cm ginger, peeled and grated
1½ green finger chillies,
   finely chopped
4 large ripe tomatoes, chopped
¾ teaspoon garam masala
1 teaspoon salt
½ teaspoon ground
   black pepper
⅓ teaspoon ground turmeric
250g peas (fresh or defrosted)
8 bread buns
a handful of chopped fresh
   coriander leaves

Preheat the oven to 180°C/350°F/gas 4.

Dust any soil from your mushrooms using kitchen paper, and break up any very large ones using your hands, then pulse in batches in the food processor until the mushrooms are chopped to lentil-size.

Put the butter and oil into a large lidded frying pan over a medium heat and, when hot, add the crushed cumin seeds and three-quarters of the red onions. Cook for around 10 minutes, then add the garlic, ginger and green chillies. Cook for another 3 minutes, then add the tomatoes and cover with the lid.

Cook for around 10 minutes, until all the water has evaporated and it looks quite thick and paste-like, then add the mushrooms. They might initially take up an alarming amount of space in the pan, but will reduce as they cook. Stir gently and cook for around 5 minutes. Add the garam masala, salt, black pepper and turmeric, and cook for another 5 minutes, then add the peas. Heat the peas through, check the salt and take off the heat.

To serve, pop the buns into the oven for 5 minutes, or until crispy. Slice off the top, hollow out the bread rolls and spoon the kheema in. Sprinkle over with fresh coriander and the remaining red onion, pop the tops back on, and eat immediately.

WILD MUSHROOMS WITH CRACKED WHEAT + CORIANDER CHUTNEY

(masaruma upma sath dhania chatni)

Wild mushoom textures and flavours vary so dramatically, it's really worth experimenting to see what you enjoy. My favourite is the ridiculously elegant chanterelle, the Chanel of the mushroom world, followed closely by the big, bulbous cep, which is meaty and looks like a sturdy seat for a little forest animal to sit on. Both work well in this upma, a well-loved and traditional South Indian breakfast dish, which I make using bulgar wheat or cracked wheat. It's spiced just delicately enough to let the mushrooms take centre stage, which is where they should be.

Serves 4 as a main course

2 cloves of garlic
1 green finger chilli
1 tablespoon lemon juice
salt
rapeseed oil
40g fresh coriander leaves
1 teaspoon black mustard seeds
10 fresh curry leaves
1 large white onion, sliced
3cm ginger, peeled and grated
200g bulgar wheat
300g chestnut mushrooms,
   sliced 1cm thick
200g wild mushrooms (e.g.
   chanterelles, ceps, enoki),
   sliced 1cm thick

First make the chutney. Bash the garlic and green chilli using a pestle and mortar until well mashed, then stir in the lemon juice, ⅓ teaspoon of salt and 3 tablespoons of oil. Finely chop the coriander and stir into the chilli garlic oil.

Boil the kettle and pour 280ml of water into a jug.

Put 2 tablespoons of oil into a lidded frying pan and, when hot, add the mustard seeds and curry leaves. When the seeds pop and the leaves crackle, add the onion and fry for around 8 minutes, until golden and starting to brown, then add the ginger and fry for a couple more minutes.

Stir in the bulgar wheat, fry for 30 seconds, then pour over the boiled water and cover with a lid. Bring to a simmer and cook for around 8 minutes, until the water evaporates, then take off the heat.

Finally, fry the mushrooms. The best way to do this is to give them a quick blast in a really hot pan – ensure they have leg room by cooking them in two or three batches, so they don't sweat on top of each other. Put 1 tablespoon of oil into a frying pan on a high heat and, when really hot, throw in your first batch. Fry any robust varieties like ceps for 3 minutes, or until burnished and tender. Fry any semi-robust mushrooms like chestnut for around 2½ minutes, and enoki, oyster or chanterelles for just 1 minute. Then transfer to the bulgar pan.

To serve, add ¾ teaspoon of salt (or to taste) to the bulgar wheat and mix in, along with most of the chutney, using the rest to decorate the top.

GUJARATI CORN ON THE COB CURRY

(gujarati makai subji)

At the age of eighty-three, my grandma has somewhat unreliable hips, but I've never seen her move so quickly to the dining table as when this curry is on the menu. It's not just one of her favourites, it's also on the A-list of curries for a lot of Gujaratis. There are no onions or garlic in this dish, but the ground peanuts, chickpea flour and yoghurt add a real depth of flavour and savoury nuttiness.

NOTE: You will need a food processor or spice grinder to grind the peanuts for this curry.

Serves 4 as a main course

120g unsalted peanuts,
    preferably red-skinned (plus
    extra to serve)
6 corn cobs
5 tablespoons rapeseed oil
60g chickpea (gram) flour
300ml Greek yoghurt
1½ teaspoons salt
½ teaspoon ground turmeric
1½ teaspoons chilli powder
1 teaspoon sugar

First grind the nuts to a fine consistency in a spice grinder or food processor and set aside.

Next, de-husk the cobs and pull off any silky strands. Make a deep horizontal cut halfway down each cob and break in half. Bring a pan of water to the boil, add the corn and boil for 6 to 8 minutes, until tender, then drain.

Put the oil into a large lidded frying pan over a low to medium heat and, once hot, add the chickpea flour, stirring continuously to smooth out any lumps. After around 4 minutes it will start to turn a pinkish brown. When it does, add the ground peanuts, turn the heat right down and cook for 5 minutes, stirring frequently.

Add the yoghurt, salt, turmeric, chilli powder and sugar to the pan. Stir to mix, then increase the heat to medium. Slowly ladle in 600ml of water, stirring until you have a smooth consistency.

Put the sweetcorn cobs into the pan, cover with the lid and leave to heat through for around 5 minutes, until the sauce is the consistency of double cream. Transfer to a serving dish or individual bowls and scatter over some crushed peanuts. Serve with rice or chapattis (see page 288) and encourage people to get stuck in with their hands.

GF

COURGETTE KOFTA IN A GINGER + TOMATO SAUCE

In Lincolnshire, the first courgettes of the season are met with wild enthusiasm, which quickly turns to apprehension because of the constant challenge of finding new and interesting ways to cook them. Over the years, this is the dish my family never tires of. The kofta are tasty by themselves, but submerged in the sauce at the last minute they make for a nice summery curry.

Serves 4 to 6 as a main course
(makes 24 kofta)

FOR THE COURGETTE KOFTA
1kg courgettes
salt
100g breadcrumbs
1 teaspoon garam masala
1 teaspoon chilli powder
1 tablespoon chickpea
    (gram) flour

FOR THE TOMATO SAUCE
rapeseed oil
2 medium brown onions, finely
    chopped
4cm ginger, peeled and grated
400g tomato passata
1 teaspoon ground cumin
1 teaspoon ground coriander
1½ teaspoons garam masala
1¼ teaspoons chilli powder
2 teaspoons honey
3 tablespoons ground almonds
1¼ teaspoons salt

Preheat the oven to 200°C/400°F/gas 6 and line two baking trays with lightly oiled foil.

Next, grate the courgettes – either in a food processor, using a grating disc, or with the coarse side of a box grater. Transfer the grated courgette to a sieve over a bowl and sprinkle with 2 teaspoons of salt. Mix well, using clean hands, and leave for 30 minutes.

In the meantime, make the tomato sauce. Put 3 tablespoons of oil into a large lidded frying pan over a medium heat and, when hot, add the onions. Cook for 8 to 10 minutes, until soft and golden, then add the ginger. Cook for a further 3 minutes, then add the tomato passata. Mix well, cover with the lid, and cook for 10 minutes, stirring occasionally. Then add the cumin, coriander, garam masala and chilli powder, and mix well. Add the honey, ground almonds and salt, and mix again. The sauce will be quite thick now, so slowly add 200ml hot water to bring it to a nice consistency, then cook for a final 5 minutes and remove from the heat.

Take a handful of courgette at a time and squeeze out as much water as you can, then transfer to another bowl. The courgettes should now weigh around 550g. Add the breadcrumbs, garam masala, chilli powder and chickpea flour and mix together. Take a golf-ball-sized bit of mixture, roll into a ball and place on a baking tray. Repeat with the rest of the mixture, then put the trays into the oven and bake for 20 minutes, until crispy on the outside. Heat the tomato sauce, carefully lever the kofta off the trays using a palette knife and drop into the sauce.

Serve with rice, and cucumber and mint raita (see page 247) or beetroot raita (page 248).

MANGALOREAN PLANTAIN CURRY

(kele ki subji)

The Mangaloreans are bananas for bananas. They eat banana buns (see page 228) for breakfast, banana chips or toffee for a late-morning snack, and for dinner they eat this plantain curry, sometimes on banana leaves.

It's best to use ripe plantains for this recipe. They tend to have a few worrying black spots on the skin but are usually perfect inside. If you can only find unripe green or yellow plantains, they will work too but will be a bit starchier and less sweet.

Serves 4 as a main course

1.2kg plantains
optional: juice of 1 lemon
2 teaspoons cumin seeds
2 teaspoons coriander seeds
2 tablespoons desiccated or
 fresh grated coconut
4 large ripe tomatoes
rapeseed or coconut oil
1 teaspoon black mustard seeds
250g shallots, thinly sliced
4 cloves of garlic, crushed
1¼ teaspoons chilli powder
¼ teaspoon ground turmeric
1⅓ teaspoons salt
200ml tinned coconut milk
15 fresh curry leaves

To prepare your plantains, cut them while they're still in their skins. Top, tail and cut into three, then halve each section. Peel just before using so they don't discolour (or peel in advance and pop them into a bowl of cold water with the lemon juice).

Place a large lidded frying pan over a medium heat and, when hot, add the cumin and coriander seeds. Stir-fry for a couple of minutes, until the cumin seeds turn a shade darker and the coriander seeds turn golden, then throw in the coconut. Stir-fry for another minute, then tip into a pestle and mortar. Grind the seeds and coconut as finely as you can.

Chop each of your tomatoes into 8 wedges. Put 2 tablespoons of oil into the same frying pan and, when hot, add the mustard seeds and shallots. Fry for 6 minutes, until the shallots are soft. Add the garlic and cook for a further 2 minutes, then add the tomato wedges. Cook for around 6 minutes, until they start to soften and collapse, then add the cumin, coriander and coconut mix, as well as the chilli powder, turmeric and salt, and stir to mix.

Peel the plantains, or drain from the lemony water if using, and add to the pan. Stir to coat with the masala, then add the coconut milk and 100ml of water – or just enough to cover the plantains. Cover with the lid and cook for 8 to 10 minutes, until the plantains are tender and a knife slips through them easily. Check the chilli and the salt levels, then take off the heat.

Transfer the curry to a serving dish. To finish, put a tablespoon of oil into a small frying pan over a medium heat and, when hot, add the curry leaves. Let them crackle and harden until they stop crackling, which will take a minute, then pour the oil and leaves over the plantain curry. Serve with rice and a fresh leafy salad.

OKRA AND POTATOES WITH TOASTED SESAME SEEDS

(aloo bhindi subji)

The recipe was inspired by some okra I ate at my favourite restaurant in Goa, called Gunpowder. It is okra and potatoes like you've never seen them, as if they've been given a glamorous Hollywood makeover: tossed in cumin seeds, curry leaves and garlic, then flavoured with tamarind and spiked with chilli before being encrusted with toasted sesame seeds. This dish goes very well with moong dal (see page 170) or an aubergine curry, alongside chapattis (page 288) or rice, and yoghurt.

NOTE: As tamarind paste varies from brand to brand, add it gradually until it tastes good to you.

Serves **4** as part
  of a main course

30g sesame seeds
2 tablespoons rapeseed oil
1 teaspoon cumin seeds
1 teaspoon black mustard seeds
10 fresh curry leaves
3 cloves of garlic, finely sliced
300g Jersey potatoes, washed,
  each cut into 6 wedges
700g okra, topped
1 teaspoon chilli flakes
1½ teaspoons tamarind paste
¼ teaspoon ground turmeric
1 teaspoon salt

First toast the sesame seeds. Set a large lidded frying pan over a medium heat and, when hot, add the seeds. Stir-fry them for 2 to 3 minutes, until almond brown, then tip on to a plate.

Put the oil into the same pan over a medium heat and, when hot, add the cumin seeds, mustard seeds and curry leaves. Stir for a minute, until the seeds pop and the curry leaves crackle, then add the garlic.

A minute later, add the potatoes and stir-fry for 3 minutes, then add 2 tablespoons of water, pop the lid on and cook for a further 5 minutes. Add the okra, turn the heat up a little, stir, pop the lid back on, and cook for 8 minutes, adding a tablespoon of water and stirring if the potatoes stick to the bottom of the pan.

Now add the chilli flakes, tamarind, turmeric, salt and sesame seeds. Stir and cover again, cooking for a further 4 minutes, or until both the potatoes and okra are tender. Check the seasoning, take off the heat and serve.

GLORIOUSLY GREEN

The arrival of summer used to send my grandfather on a buying spree. He'd ask one of his sons to warm up the big van while he finished his ritual of polishing his patent leather shoes, brushing down his wool suit and dabbing a little jasmine perfume behind his ears. Then he was ready to go. He'd drive down to a wholesale Indian vegetable market in Leicester and stock up on new-season greens, or 'shaak bhaji'. He loved it. If I went with him, I would watch as he gleefully danced around the different crates of produce. To me it was a cold, dark, dusty warehouse, but to him, it was paradise. He would marvel at the wide, robust leaves of the mustard greens, be thrilled by the sight of the first baby okra, gasp when he saw his favourite, baby ivy gourd, and he would stuff flat beans into bags as if they were rare and precious jewels. He knew just how much prepping and cooking my grandmother could stand to do later that day, and he knew the exact capacity of the freezer to hold his surplus trophy buys.

We didn't have an Indian market near where I grew up in Lincolnshire. Mostly I remember the endless kindness of our neighbours, Aunty Sheila and Uncle Raymond, who would drop by with a bag of whatever was bursting out of their allotment. In the spring there would be purple sprouting broccoli; in the summer, there would be beans and little courgettes; then, in the winter, savoy cabbages.

Mum and I learned how to cook all of these greens over time: quickly, just long enough to keep the colour and the crunch for optimum flavour, and never to over-spice or over-sauce these delicate things.

Over the years, I've discovered a few favourite flavours and techniques: for example, Brussels sprouts shredded and quickly fried are a completely different beast from their boiled counterparts, and work well with Keralan flavours – lime, shallots, coconut and chillies. Tandoori broccoli with a classic Malai marinade of cream cheese and cardamom, roasted until charred, is divine (see page 84).

My great-grandfather used to grow asparagus back in Gujarat, and served them as a fresh pickle, thinly sliced with lemon juice and salt. I adore them like this, but for something more substantial I cook them briefly (tips raw) in a classic Bengali mustard sauce usually reserved for fish (page 109). My grandfather loved them so much that when he died, my mother put a bunch under his arm.

Today I buy whatever is in season at my local market, Chapel Market, in London and, like my grandfather, I buy too much, cook too much and freeze whatever is left over to enjoy when the season has gone.

ROASTED BROCCOLI WITH ALMONDS + CARDAMOM

(malai broccoli)

I first ate this dish when out with friends at a restaurant called Chulha in Goa. One bite and the conversation faded while this broccoli and I had a real moment together. The key to making this dish great is cramming the mixture into the nooks and crannies of the broccoli florets and not being afraid to char the edges.

Serves 6 as a side

750g broccoli florets
220g cream cheese
1 teaspoon ground black pepper
¾ teaspoon ground cardamom
   (or finely ground seeds from
   8 pods)
1 teaspoon salt
⅓ of a whole nutmeg, grated
4 tablespoons Greek yoghurt
75g ground almonds
3 tablespoons lemon juice

Preheat the oven to 200°C/400°F/gas 6 and line two large baking trays with baking paper.

Break the florets into bite-sized pieces. Place all the ingredients except the florets in a bowl and mix well. Then add the florets and mix with your hands – make sure the mixture gets into all the nooks and crannies of the broccoli.

Roast for 10 minutes, turn the pieces over and cook for a further 10 minutes, or until the broccoli is tender, crunchy and charred in places.

Pile the broccoli up high in a bowl or on a plate and serve.

GF

HARA BARA KEBABS
WITH BURNT LIME RAITA

One of my favourite places in Mumbai is Chor Bazaar, or Thieves Market. It used to be where the vagabonds and villains in the city would offload their stolen loot. These days you can find ancient tiffin tins and all sorts of knick-knacks there, and right in the midst there's a man with the best hara bara kebabs I've ever eaten. Packed full of as many greens, or 'hara', as he can stuff into them, they're soft and charred but bright with fresh herbs, chilli and lemon. I've tried to re-create them here as best I can.

Makes **18 kebabs**
(enough for 4 to 6)

FOR THE RAITA
250ml Greek yoghurt
1 tablespoon rapeseed oil
1 lime, quartered
⅓ teaspoon salt
1 teaspoon honey or sugar
1 teaspoon nigella seeds

FOR THE KEBABS
500g white mashing potatoes
   such as Maris Piper or
   King Edwards
1½ teaspoons cumin seeds
2 green finger chillies
3.5cm ginger, peeled
200g spinach leaves
200g peas (fresh or defrosted)
2 tablespoons chickpea
   (gram) flour
1 tablespoon lemon juice
1⅓ teaspoons salt
2 teaspoons garam masala
3 tablespoons finely chopped
   fresh coriander leaves
rapeseed oil

First make the lime raita. Put the yoghurt into a bowl. Put the oil into a small frying pan over a medium heat and, when hot, add the lime wedges. Fry for a minute on each side, or until the sides have blackened and become sticky, then take off the heat. When the wedges have cooled, squeeze the juice into the yoghurt, add the salt and honey or sugar, and stir to mix. Garnish with the nigella seeds, and a squeezed slice of lime if you feel like it, then refrigerate until needed.

Wash and peel the potatoes, then place in a saucepan. Cover with cold water and boil until completely tender, then drain and mash well. While the potatoes are boiling, bash the cumin seeds coarsely with a pestle and mortar, then transfer to a small bowl. Grind together the green chillies and ginger in the pestle and mortar until they both disintegrate, and mix with the cumin. Wash the spinach and bring some fresh water to the boil. Gently dunk the spinach in for a minute, then drain and refresh under the cold tap for 30 seconds. When cool enough to handle, squeeze out as much water as possible (don't be afraid to be brutish), then chop finely and add to the mashed potatoes.

Next, add the peas, the cumin, ginger and green chilli paste, the chickpea flour, lemon juice, salt, garam masala and coriander to the potato mixture. Knead with your hands until all the ingredients are well mixed, then cook a test kebab. Put 2 tablespoons of oil into a large frying pan over a medium heat. Take a golf-ball-sized bit of mixture, shape into a ball between your palms and flatten it to roughly 6cm in diameter and 2cm thick. Fry for 2½ minutes on one side, or until golden and crisp, then flip and cook for a further 2½ minutes. Once crisp and golden on both sides, remove with a slotted spoon.

Cool, and taste for salt and lemon, adjusting if need be. Then fry the rest in batches, adding a little oil where you need it to stop the kebabs from sticking to the pan. Keep the cooked kebabs warm in a foil nest, then serve them together with the raita.

GF

KERALAN VEGETABLE ISTOO

Take a journey to Kerala using vegetables from an English allotment. If you like your curries to be gentle and flavourful but light and packed full of vitality, this is the one is for you. You can use 1kg of any mixed vegetables for this dish, but just remember to cook the hardest first (e.g. potatoes) and the softest last (e.g. peas), so nothing ends up over- or undercooked.

Serves 4 as a main course

250g baby new potatoes
250g broccoli
2 medium carrots
   (about 200g)
200g green beans
4 tablespoons rapeseed oil
4 cloves
4cm cinnamon stick
12 black peppercorns
optional: 12 fresh curry leaves
1 large onion, finely diced
3cm ginger, peeled and grated
3 cloves of garlic, crushed
1½ green finger chillies, very
   finely chopped
1 x 400ml tin of coconut milk
⅓ teaspoon ground turmeric
1 teaspoon salt (or to taste)
100g peas (fresh or defrosted)

Cut the baby potatoes into quarters, then cut the broccoli into florets the same size as the potatoes and leave in a separate pile. Peel the carrots and cut into batons, then top and tail the green beans.

Put 3 tablespoons of oil into a large lidded frying pan over a medium heat and, when hot, add the cloves, cinnamon stick, peppercorns, and curry leaves if using. When the peppercorns swell, add the onion and sweat for around 8 minutes, until soft, then add the ginger, garlic and green chillies and cook for a couple of minutes.

Now add the coconut milk, 100ml of water, the turmeric, salt and potatoes. Bring to the boil, then reduce to a simmer, cover with the lid and leave to cook for 5 minutes. Add the carrots and simmer for a further 5 minutes, or until the vegetables are very nearly tender. Add the beans and broccoli and cook for a further 3 minutes or so, then pop in the peas and heat through for a final minute.

Delicious with the tamarind and caramelized red onion rice on page 192.

SHREDDED BRUSSELS SPROUT THORAN

(choti gobhi thoran)

A thoran is a sort of quick Keralan stir-fry. Here it involves cooking shredded sprouts hard and fast, then tossing them with some sweet onions and the lively flavours of curry leaves, chilli, lemon and coconut. This is Kerala, via wintry England, on a plate.

This dish goes well with other Keralan dishes like beetroot pachadi (see page 51) or tamarind and caramelized red onion rice (page 192).

Serves 4 to 6 as a side

600g Brussels sprouts, washed
2 tablespoons coconut oil
1 teaspoon black mustard seeds
12 fresh curry leaves
1 large red onion, thinly sliced
2 cloves of garlic, crushed
1 red chilli, finely sliced
50g desiccated or fresh
  grated coconut
⅔ teaspoon salt
juice of ½ a lemon

First shred the sprouts. The easiest way to do this is in a food processor fitted with a 2mm slicing disc. If you don't have a food processor, slice them as thinly as you can by hand.

Put the coconut oil into a wide-bottomed pan over a medium to high heat. When hot, add the mustard seeds and curry leaves. Wait for them to sizzle and pop, then add the red onion.

Cook until soft and starting to caramelize, then add the garlic, red chilli and coconut. Stir-fry for a couple of minutes until the raw smell of the garlic disappears, then turn the heat up, add the sprouts and mix thoroughly.

Keep tossing and turning for 4 minutes, then add the salt and lemon juice. Cook for a further 2 minutes, then take off the heat. Taste to check the salt and lemon balance, and adjust if need be.

GRILLED SWEETHEART CABBAGE + COCONUT THORAN

(gobhi ka thoran)

Ben Benton is one of the greatest chefs I know. This is his recipe, and although he is not Keralan, he has a tremendous ability to get under the skin of the cuisine. He taught me that by chargrilling the cut sides of cabbage a whole new side of its personality is revealed: the layers within become sweet and tender. Then, tossed with lime and coconut, it becomes lively – a great side to eat with a spiced rice dish, or with crab or shrimp.

Serves **4 as a side**

100g fresh coconut,
  or 80g desiccated
½ a red onion, very finely diced
1.5cm ginger, peeled and
  finely grated
2 large ripe tomatoes,
  finely diced
1 teaspoon chilli powder
1 tablespoon lime juice
⅓ teaspoon salt
2 sweetheart or pointed
  cabbages (800g in total)
rapeseed or coconut oil

First make the coconut and tomato salad. If you're using fresh coconut, pop it into a blender to shred it, or grate it with a box grater, and put into a bowl. If you're using desiccated coconut, pour 40ml of boiling water over the coconut, leave for a couple of minutes, then fluff up using a fork. Add the red onion, ginger, tomatoes, chilli powder, lime juice and salt. Mix well and leave to one side.

To cook the cabbages, first quarter them lengthways, then brush each side with oil. Put a large griddle pan or frying pan over a medium heat. Wait until the pan is really hot – the cabbage should sizzle when it goes on – then add the wedges. You might need to cook them in batches.

Grill for 10 to 12 minutes, until lightly charred and tender on both sides, turning every couple of minutes. Then throw in the coconut and tomato mixture and gently toss to warm through for a couple of heartbeats.

Serve the cabbage piled on a plate, topped with the warm coconut and tomato mixture.

SAVOY CABBAGE, BLACK KALE + POTATO SUBJI

(savoy aloo gobhi)

In Gujarat, cabbages and potatoes are near deities. In Lincolnshire, where they are the main crops, the same is true. I feel as though my bones, and the bones of my ancestors, are partly made up of these two vegetables. When you want something simple, not much beats a tangle of soft buttery cabbage with sweet caramelized onions and crisp potatoes, alongside a fierce pickle, yoghurt and chapattis (see page 288).

Serves **4 to 6 as part**
of a main course

1 teaspoon coriander seeds
2 teaspoons cumin seeds
3 tablespoons rapeseed oil
15 fresh curry leaves
1 teaspoon black mustard seeds
1 large brown onion, halved and
  thinly sliced
800g baby new potatoes,
  quartered
200g savoy cabbage, finely
  shredded
200g black kale or cavalo nero,
  finely shredded
1¼ teaspoons salt
½ teaspoon chilli powder
¾ teaspoon ground turmeric

Lightly grind the coriander and cumin seeds with a pestle and mortar. Put the oil into a large lidded frying pan over a medium heat and, when hot, add the curry leaves and mustard seeds. When they crackle, add the onion. Cook for around 10 minutes, until golden and sweet, stirring occasionally.

Add the crushed coriander and cumin, followed by the potatoes. Cook for 10 minutes, turning every now and then until crispy. Add a couple of tablespoons of water, cover with the lid and cook for a further 5 minutes, until the potatoes are tender and no longer resist the point of a knife.

Finally, add the shredded cabbage and black kale to the pan with a couple of tablespoons of water and stir-fry for 3 minutes. Add the salt, chilli and turmeric, mix well, cover with the lid, reduce the heat to low and cook for another 4 minutes, or until the cabbage and black kale have wilted.

Serve with a fiery pickle, hot chapattis and a dollop of yoghurt, or alongside dal and rice.

FENUGREEK LEAVES, PEAS + CREAM

(methi matar malai)

Indian supermarkets can look pretty intimidating to the uninitiated – packed full of odd fruits and weird brands. On my list of recommended things to buy would be fenugreek. It's a bitter leaf with a strong taste that transforms into something discreet and magical when balanced with other flavours, like creamy cashews and sweet peas. You can spot it either by its heart-shaped (purslane-esque) leaves, or by its smell, which is somewhere between maple syrup and liquorice. In fact, rumour has it that if you're on the London to Bristol train, you can smell fenugreek round about Southall.

NOTES: This recipe uses amchur (mango powder), also available from your local Indian shop. You will need a blender for this recipe.

Serves **4 as part of a main course**

50g unsalted cashews
300g fresh fenugreek leaves
salt
4cm ginger, peeled
2 green finger chillies
40g unsalted butter
6 medium ripe tomatoes, chopped
1 teaspoon garam masala
1 teaspoon mango powder (amchur)
1 teaspoon sugar
150ml single cream
200g frozen petit pois

Soak the cashews in 150ml of boiled water for 10 minutes.

In the meantime, wash the fenugreek, cut off the stalks below where the leaves grow, and discard, as they are very tough when cooked. Finely chop the leaves and soak them in a large bowl of cold water with a big pinch of salt for 10 minutes. This will help to extract some of their bitterness.

Put the cashews, their soaking water, the ginger and green chillies into a blender and whizz into a smooth paste.

Put the butter into a lidded frying pan over a medium heat and, when hot, add the tomatoes. Cook them for around 5 minutes, until they break down, stirring every couple of minutes. Then add the garam masala, mango powder, sugar and 1¼ teaspoons of salt. Stir to mix, then grab a handful at a time of the fenugreek leaves, shake off the water and add to the pan. Cover with a lid and cook for 6 to 8 minutes, until tender.

Add the cashew paste and cook for a couple of minutes, then add the cream and peas.

Cover the pan again and cook for a further 5 minutes. Check for seasoning, and serve with bread or rice.

GF

STOLEN MUSTARD GREENS

(sarson ka saag)

Many a time when I was growing up, my mum would tell my dad to stop the car alongside a mustard field in Lincolnshire while she ran in, gleefully bounced around and stole some leaves for dinner. In her defence, back then no one but Indians really ate these leaves, so this was the only way of getting hold of them. Now, they're available in a lot of big supermarkets, farmers' markets and Asian shops, so she's stopped her naughty ways.

If you've never had mustard greens, you're in for a treat. They're more flavourful than spinach, and more comforting. They're traditionally eaten with corn roti (see page 217), and butter made from freshly churned cream (page 285). Home-made butter isn't essential, but boy, oh boy, is it good.

NOTE: You will need a blender for this recipe.

Serves **4 as a main course**

1kg mustard leaves
3 tablespoons rapeseed oil
2 large brown onions,
    finely chopped
5cm ginger, peeled
6 cloves of garlic, crushed
2 green finger chillies,
    finely sliced
3 tablespoons cornmeal
1½ teaspoons salt
20g unsalted butter

First clean the mustard leaves of any sand or dirt. Put them into a large bowl of cold water and wash them a couple of times, then shake them under the water so all the grit falls to the bottom. Don't drain, just pull the leaves out of the water a small bunch at a time (making sure they're clean), then cut them into 5cm strips. Put the cut greens into a large saucepan as you go.

Add around 500ml of cold water to the pan, cover with a lid and bring to the boil. Turn the heat down and simmer for 15 minutes, or until the leaves are completely tender. Then liquidize the greens in a blender, using only as much water as you need (around 4 tablespoons) to form a lovely thick consistency.

In the meantime, put the oil into a frying pan over a medium heat. When hot, add the onions and cook until they are translucent. Cut 4cm of the ginger into tiny cubes, and 1cm into matchsticks. Add the cubed ginger, crushed garlic, green chillies and cornmeal to the pan and cook for 5 minutes.

Next, add the greens to the pan, along with the salt and butter, turn the heat to low and cook for 8 minutes, adding water as you wish to adjust the consistency. It should be the consistency of hummus.

Serve hot, scattered with the remaining, matchsticked ginger, alongside corn roti and as much butter as your arteries will allow.

RAINBOW CHARD SAAG ALOO

I'll never forget my mum's head-turning squeal when she saw a bag of Desiree potatoes marked 'grown in Lincolnshire' in the aisle of a London supermarket. She's evangelical about their butteriness, and proud of the fact they're grown near our family home, so this dish, which uses a classic Gujarati spicing of cumin, coriander, turmeric and chilli, appears regularly on the Sodha family table.

Serves 2 to 3 as a main course

400g rainbow or Swiss chard
3 tablespoons rapeseed oil
1 teaspoon black mustard seeds
2 medium brown onions, sliced
600g Desiree potatoes
3cm ginger, peeled and grated
4 cloves of garlic, crushed
400g ripe tomatoes, cut
  into wedges
1⅓ teaspoons chilli powder
⅓ teaspoon ground cumin
⅓ teaspoon ground coriander
½ teaspoon ground turmeric
1¼ teaspoons salt

To prepare the chard, cut the stems from the leaves. Cut the stems into 4cm pieces and slice the leaves into 4cm strips.

Put the oil into a large lidded frying pan and, when hot, add the mustard seeds. When they pop, add the onions and cook for 12 to 15 minutes, until soft and golden brown. In the meantime, peel the potatoes and cut into 2cm cubes. When the onions are ready, add the ginger and garlic to the pan and cook for a couple of minutes, then add the potatoes and 200ml of water. Cover and cook for 10 minutes.

Add the tomatoes and the chard stalks, cover and cook for a further 5 minutes, or until the chard stalks are soft. Add the chilli, cumin, coriander, turmeric and salt and stir gently. Finally, add the chard leaves, coat with the mixture and pop the lid back on for a final 2 to 3 minutes, until the leaves have wilted.

Serve with hot chapattis (see page 288) or rice, yoghurt and a little pickle.

SPINACH, TOMATO + CHICKPEA CURRY

(chana saag)

When I think of this dish, and how the words 'chana saag' are now familiar to so many British people, it makes me thankful for all the Bangladeshis who first came here from Kolkata at the end of the British Raj. Many of them jumped into the restaurant trade, keen to bring Indian dishes, popular with Brits in India, to our high streets. It's thanks to them that chana saag is (almost) as popular here as it is in India.

This is my take on the classic. It's a bit perkier than your average curry-house chana saag, and uses just-wilted spinach.

Serves 4 as a main course

3 tablespoons rapeseed oil
½ teaspoon black
  mustard seeds
1 teaspoon cumin seeds
2 large onions, diced
5 cloves of garlic, crushed
2cm ginger, peeled and grated
1 x 400g tin of plum tomatoes
2 x 400g tin of
  chickpeas, drained
1½ teaspoons ground coriander
1 teaspoon chilli powder
½ teaspoon ground turmeric
1 teaspoon salt
500g baby spinach, washed

Put the oil into a large lidded pan over a medium heat and, when hot, add the mustard seeds and cumin seeds. Stir for a minute, or until they pop, then throw in the onions.

Fry for 10 to 12 minutes, until they turn translucent and start to caramelize, then add the garlic and ginger. Stir-fry for around 3 minutes, then add the tinned tomatoes, pouring them in with one hand and crushing them with the other. Fill the empty tin a third of the way up with water and add that to the pan too.

Cook for 10 minutes, until quite dry and paste-like, then add the chickpeas. Warm them for a couple of minutes, then add the coriander, chilli powder, turmeric and salt. Toss the chickpeas around in the paste, and add the spinach – trying to fold it all in will be like pushing a duvet into a magical handbag, but it will wilt and shrink fairly quickly.

Cook for around 5 minutes, until the spinach is soft and tender, and serve with chapattis (see page 288) or basmati rice, and a dollop of yoghurt.

RUNNER BEAN SUBJI

When the first valor beans of the season arrive in Gujarat, women sit cross-legged around a pyramid of them and twist, peel and pod, chatting and giggling as they do so. Valor beans don't grow in the UK, but runner beans do, and when their season arrives, my aunts and mum prepare them in the same way, around the kitchen table.

This is a simple summer subji, an everyday vegetable dish that is lovely with bread and yoghurt, and tastier if prepared by your aunts. It also goes well with aubergines, like the aubergine and pea curry on page 118, and rice.

Serves **4** as part
 of a main course

750g runner beans
2 tablespoons rapeseed oil
optional: 15 fresh curry leaves
1 teaspoon black mustard seeds
4 cloves of garlic, thinly sliced
1 green finger chilli,
 thinly sliced
3cm ginger, peeled and grated
6 banana shallots, finely sliced
150g baby plum tomatoes (or just
 good, ripe toms), chopped
½ teaspoon ground turmeric
¾ teaspoon salt (or to taste)
½ teaspoon ground
 black pepper

Wash your beans, top and tail them, then peel away the sides using a vegetable peeler to remove the tough fibrous strings. Cut them on a diagonal into 4cm pieces.

Put the oil into a large lidded frying pan and, when hot, add the curry leaves (if using) and mustard seeds. When they start to crackle, add the garlic, green chilli and ginger. Stir-fry for 2 minutes, then add the shallots and cook for around 12 to 15 minutes, until golden and caramelized.

Next, add the tomatoes and cook for a couple of minutes, then add the turmeric, salt and black pepper, and stir to mix. Throw in the beans and a few tablespoons of water, stir and pop the lid on.

Cook the beans for 6 to 8 minutes, until they're soft and have just lost their crunch, then serve fresh and hot.

ASPARAGUS + PEAS IN A BENGALI MUSTARD SAUCE

In England, we usually treat mustard as a condiment – highly dangerous and to be eaten in small quantities. But in Bengal they make wonderful dishes using mustard in large amounts, as the lead flavour. In this recipe, the mustard and yoghurt come together to make a pungent and rich sauce which doesn't overpower but instead complements the sweet, clean flavours of the peas and asparagus.

Although Bengalis tend to grind their own mustard seeds, I've used ready-made English mustard in this recipe, which is simpler and works a treat. Eat with either buttered naan, or buttery moong dal (see page 170) and rice.

NOTE: You will need a blender for this recipe.

Serves **4 as part
of a main course**

2 tablespoons Colman's
 mustard
1 green finger chilli
2 tablespoons lemon juice
3 cloves of garlic, peeled
2cm ginger, peeled
150ml Greek yoghurt
2 tablespoons desiccated or
 fresh grated coconut
2 tablespoons rapeseed oil
½ teaspoon cumin seeds
½ teaspoon black mustard
 seeds
1 red onion, diced
400g asparagus, cut into
 2cm pieces
400g peas (fresh or defrosted)
½ teaspoon salt

First make the mustard paste. Put the mustard, green chilli, lemon juice, garlic, ginger, yoghurt and coconut into a blender and pulse to a fine paste.

Next, put the oil into a large frying pan and, when hot, add the cumin and mustard seeds. When the seeds start to wriggle in the oil, add the red onion and cook for around 8 minutes, until soft and translucent. Then turn the heat down and add the mustard paste.

Stir the mustard paste for a couple of minutes so that it doesn't split, then turn the heat up to medium and add all the asparagus, except for the tips. Cook for 2 minutes, then add the peas and cook for a further 2 minutes. Add the asparagus tips, cook for a final 30 seconds to a minute, then take off the heat. Season with the salt and serve.

AUBERGINES

My first love was the aubergine. When other mothers were busy playing snakes and ladders with their children, mine was showing me (at the tender age of eight) how to buy the perfect aubergine: bright green top, very taut skin, and a hollow sound when tapped (which suggests fewer seeds, according to my mum).

Aubergines may be a fruit, but they wouldn't be caught dead in your fruit bowl: they prefer to be partnered with the bold flavours of tomatoes and onions, which play up the aubergine's creamy subtlety.

When raw, the flesh is bouncy and absorbent like a sponge, greedily sucking up any oil or sauce nearby. This is always somewhat worrying and has led to many debates about how best to prepare and cook aubergines. More often than not, I will cook them in a little liquid or a sauce, as in the aubergine and pea curry on page 118, or the coal-smoked aubergine curry on page 116. In this way, they steam and stew and eventually soften and collapse into a lovely scoopable texture – and no extra oil is needed to cook them in.

Occasionally, I will roast aubergines until they collapse, as I've done in the aubergine fesenjan on page 115, or pan-fry sliced aubergine in batches in a small amount of oil, because I find the crispiness on the outside, along with the creaminess inside, completely irresistible.

Some people suggest salting aubergine slices ahead of time – not only to remove any bitterness, but also to remove some of the water content, which in theory means they will cook more quickly, therefore needing less oil. I don't do this, however – partly because if I'm genuinely concerned about the amount of oil, I'll cook the aubergine until the water evaporates and skim off the oil at the end. I've also never encountered any off-putting bitterness in aubergines. It may just be that modern varieties are less bitter.

Disappointingly, you can only usually find one variety – or at best two – in supermarket aisles, but the aubergine is in fact quite a family. The ones I use most often are the large and most commonly available sort, many of which are grown in Holland. Second to that I'll buy the small, round, baby purple aubergines which fit perfectly in the palm of your hand. We Gujaratis stuff these with coconut and peanuts and steam them until they collapse (see page 112); these are also the aubergines I use in the chutney on page 233. My mother prefers the small thin purple Bengali aubergines because she says they have fewer seeds and a more intense flavour. They can be cooked in the same way as any of the other aubergines, although won't take as long to cook as they're slimmer.

BABY AUBERGINES STUFFED WITH PEANUT + COCONUT

(bhara baingan)

Two years ago I went to Kanora in Gujarat to visit the birthplace of my grandfather. I asked around for the old Lakhani house. A village elder pointed it out. I knocked on the door tentatively and was welcomed in by the new owners. The smell coming from the kitchen was magical: they were making this dish– aubergines cooked in peanut and coconut, a Gujarati classic – and they invited me to stay for lunch. I sat at the kitchen table where my grandfather would have sat with his brother and seven sisters, and imagined what he must have been thinking when he decided to set sail across the Arabian Sea to seek his fortune in Africa. In all the years I knew him, I never thought to ask him about it. But I did on many occasions share this dish with him, and every time I eat it, it reminds me to dream big.

NOTE: You will need a food processor for this recipe.

Serves **4 as a main course**

12 baby aubergines (800g)
60g desiccated or
  fresh grated coconut
120g roasted unsalted peanuts
40g fresh coriander
8 cloves of garlic
1 green finger chilli
2 tablespoons tomato puree
1 teaspoon ground cumin
¾ teaspoon ground turmeric
1 teaspoon sugar
1¾ teaspoons salt
3 tablespoons rapeseed oil
1 large onion, sliced

Cut each aubergine in half lengthways, but don't cut through the stem. Roll each one over and cut lengthways again, still keeping the stem intact. Put into a bowl of cold water and set aside.

Put a large lidded frying pan over a medium heat and, when hot, toast the coconut and peanuts for 2 to 3 minutes, until the coconut is starting to brown. Tip into a bowl and leave to cool. Put the coriander, garlic, green chilli, tomato puree, cumin, turmeric, sugar and salt into a food processor, along with the cooled peanuts and coconut. Pulse until coarsely ground and fully mixed.

Open each aubergine out like a flower and fill with the coconut mixture, using your hands. Roll the aubergine over, open and stuff again, then press closed. If there's any leftover stuffing, add it to the pan later, when you cook the aubergines.

Next, put the oil into the frying pan over a medium heat. When hot, add the onion and fry until golden and soft. Add the aubergines and 2 tablespoons of water, turn the heat up high and cook for a couple of minutes, then put the lid on and turn the heat down. Cook for 10 minutes, then gently turn the aubergines and add a splash of water if they're looking dry. Cook for a further 20 minutes, or until nice and tender. Serve with cucumber and mint raita (see page 247), or with a salad, some yoghurt and rice or chapattis (page 288).

GF DF VE

AUBERGINE FESENJAN

The first time I met my husband was in his kitchen. He was standing amid a mountain of empty pomegranate shells and the kitchen looked like a crime scene, with red juice splattered up the walls. He wanted to impress me with this fesenjan, a dish that was often found on the tables of Indian Mughal emperors in the 1500s and 1600s but originally from Persia. Luckily, these days you can buy pomegranate molasses – which is what I told him (and it broke the ice). We got married last summer and now cook this dish together with good memories and much less mess.

NOTE: You will need a food processor to grind the walnuts.

Serves 4 as a main course

120g walnuts
4 medium aubergines (1.2 kg)
rapeseed oil
salt and ground black pepper
2 large red onions, thinly sliced
2 cloves of garlic, crushed
1½ tablespoons honey
¾ teaspoon chilli powder
1 teaspoon ground cinnamon
2 tablespoons pomegranate
    molasses
250ml hot vegetable stock
seeds from 1 pomegranate (see
    page 289 for how to deseed)
a handful of fresh coriander

Preheat the oven to 200°C/400°F/gas 6 and line a large baking tray with lightly oiled foil. Blitz the walnuts in a food processor to a fine crumb and leave to one side.

Cut the aubergines into 5cm x 2cm batons, toss with oil, season lightly with salt and black pepper, and roast on the baking tray for 25 minutes or until meltingly soft.

While the aubergines are roasting, make the fesenjan sauce. Put 3 tablespoons of oil into a large frying pan over a medium heat and, when hot, add the red onions. Fry for 12 minutes, stirring regularly to ensure they don't burn, then add the garlic and fry for a further 3 minutes.

Add the honey, chilli powder, cinnamon, ½ teaspoon of salt, 1 teaspoon of black pepper, the blitzed walnuts and the pomegranate molasses to the pan, and stir thoroughly to mix. Then add the vegetable stock and cook for around 8 minutes, until the sauce comes together.

When the aubergines are tender, pour the sauce into a serving dish. Put the aubergines on top, and scatter with the pomegranate seeds and coriander. Serve alongside steamed basmati rice.

COAL-SMOKED AUBERGINE CURRY

(baingan bharta)

As the summer starts to disappear, and with it any hope of having a barbecue, think of this recipe. It uses the classic and ancient Indian *dhungar* method of smoking food by placing a smouldering piece of charcoal in the centre of the curry and pouring a little oil over it, then covering for a minute so that the smoky flavours permeate. Close your eyes and you could be in a street market in Delhi, just without the cows.

In order to cook this dish safely, it's best to smoke it outside – i.e. when you've burned the coal, place it in the pan and carry it outside, so that no smoke enters your house. Only ever use natural lumpwood charcoal to smoke with, as it's a natural form of wood charcoal.

Serves **4 to 6 as a side**

4 tablespoons rapeseed oil
    (plus 1 teaspoon for smoking)
2 medium white onions, sliced
5 cloves of garlic, crushed
3cm ginger, peeled and grated
3 medium aubergines (900g),
    cut into 5cm x 2cm batons
4 large ripe tomatoes, cut
    into wedges
1¼ teaspoons chilli powder
1 teaspoon salt
⅓ teaspoon ground turmeric
1 teaspoon ground coriander
1 teaspoon ground cumin
a piece of charcoal around
    2cm x 2cm

Put the 4 tablespoons of oil into a large lidded frying pan over a medium heat. When hot, add the onions and fry for around 10 minutes, until soft and beginning to brown. Add the garlic and ginger and fry for 2 to 3 minutes, until the raw smell of the garlic disappears.

Next add the aubergines, along with 6 tablespoons of water, stir and pop the lid on the pan. Cook for around 15 minutes, until the aubergine pieces have collapsed, stirring very occasionally. Add the tomato wedges, chilli powder, salt, turmeric, coriander and cumin, cook for 3 to 4 minutes with the lid off, until the tomatoes become jammy around the edges, then take the pan off the heat.

To smoke the curry, place a little heatproof bowl in the centre of the pan. Hold the charcoal in a pair of tongs over a small flame until the edges burn white and red. Then place it carefully in the small bowl, put the lid over the pan and carefully carry outdoors, along with the oil for smoking and a pair of tongs. Place the pan down, open the lid, pour the teaspoon of oil over the hot coal and close the lid again to trap the smoke. For a subtle smoky flavour, smoke the curry for 1 minute. For a nicely smoked flavour, smoke for 2 minutes. Remove the bowl using the tongs and run it under a tap to extinguish the coal.

Taste the curry for chilli and salt. Adjust if need be, then serve with rice or buttery naan bread and yoghurt.

AUBERGINE + PEA CURRY

(baingan matar masala)

When I got back from my honeymoon, I spoke to my grandma.
  'Are you happily married?' she asked.
  'Yes, Grandma.'
  'What have you eaten today?'
  'Aubergine and pea curry and chapattis.'
  'Good. If you're eating properly, you must be happy.'

Serves **4** as a main course

5 tablespoons rapeseed oil
1 teaspoon cumin seeds
2 large onions, finely chopped
6 cloves of garlic, crushed
4 large ripe tomatoes, chopped
1½ tablespoons tomato puree
1½ level teaspoons salt
1¼ teaspoons chilli powder
½ teaspoon ground turmeric
1 teaspoon sugar
4 medium aubergines (1.2kg),
  chopped into 3cm cubes
100g peas (fresh or defrosted)

Put the oil into a wide-bottomed lidded pan over a medium heat. Once hot, add the cumin seeds, stir for 30 seconds, then add the onions.

Cook for around 10 minutes, until the onions are soft and translucent but not brown, then add the garlic and stir-fry for a couple of minutes. Add the chopped tomatoes and tomato puree, and cover with a lid. Leave to cook for 5 minutes, then add the salt, chilli powder, turmeric and sugar.

Now add the aubergines, coating the pieces with the masala, pop the lid back on the pan and cook for around 10 minutes. You want the aubergines to be tender and soft with little to no water running from them – if they're watery, or not yet tender, they may need another few minutes' cooking.

When they're cooked, add the peas and cook for a couple of minutes, then take off the heat. Serve with hot chapattis (see page 288) or rice.

(AUBERGINES)

 GF DF VE

SESAME + TAMARIND AUBERGINES WITH CRACKED WHEAT

The people of Andhra Pradesh love their pungent, spicy and sour flavours, as well as cooking vegetables in rich pastes made of sesame seeds, poppy seeds or peanuts. This dish is typical of the region and uses tamarind for sourness and sesame seeds for rich creaminess. I've borrowed the cracked wheat from Andhra's neighbouring state Hyderabad to serve the aubergines with.

NOTES: You will need a blender for this recipe. As tamarind paste varies from brand to brand, add it gradually until it tastes good to you.

Serves 4 as a main course

2 large ripe tomatoes
2 tablespoons sesame seeds
3 cloves of garlic
2 teaspoons tamarind paste
1 teaspoon ground cumin
1 teaspoon ground coriander
1½ teaspoons chilli powder
salt
2 tablespoons rapeseed oil
1 large onion, sliced
3 medium aubergines (900g),
   cut into 6cm x 2cm batons
200g bulgar wheat
100ml Greek yoghurt
10g fresh mint leaves

Place the tomatoes, sesame seeds, garlic, tamarind paste, cumin, coriander, chilli powder and a teaspoon of salt into a blender, whizz to a sauce and leave to one side.

Put the oil into a large lidded frying pan over a medium heat. When hot, add the onion and fry for 10 to 12 minutes, until soft and golden. Add the sauce to the pan, cook for a couple of minutes, then add the aubergines and 5 tablespoons of water. Stir to mix, then cover the pan and cook for 15 minutes, or until the aubergines are soft and tender, adding a splash of water if need be to stop them from sticking.

In the meantime, cook the bulgar wheat. Place the wheat into a heatproof bowl or lidded saucepan and cover with 280ml of freshly boiled water. Add ¼ teaspoon of salt, cover with a lid, and leave to fluff up for around 8 minutes.

To serve, transfer the bulgar wheat to a serving dish, top with the aubergines, dot with the yoghurt, and tear up and scatter over the mint.

HUMAYUN'S AUBERGINE KUKU

Humayun was a Mughal emperor in Delhi in the 1500s. He earned the title 'Perfect Man' for his patience and tranquillity, and he was partial to refined Persian food, cooked by the best chefs of his day. When he wasn't eating stuffed roasted whole sheep, or all-white-food feasts, he was fond of this kuku, a gorgeous herby aubergine frittata. In the 1500s they ate this with yoghurt and I wouldn't disagree with that, but a little salad, pickle and crusty bread are also lovely alongside.

Serves **4 to 6 as a light lunch**

2 medium aubergines
  (about 600g)
rapeseed oil
100g spring onions,
  finely sliced
2 cloves of garlic, crushed
1 teaspoon salt
6 medium eggs
½ teaspoon ground
  black pepper
20g fresh dill, leaves picked

Chop the aubergines into 1cm x 5cm batons.

Pour 80ml of oil into a large frying pan over a medium heat and, when hot, add the aubergines. At first they will soak up all the oil, but will eventually start to release it back into the pan. After 10 to 12 minutes, when you can see the oil and the aubergines are lovely and soft, add the spring onions, garlic and ½ teaspoon of salt, and mix together. Take off the heat and leave to cool for 5 minutes.

In the meantime, beat the eggs and season with the remaining ½ teaspoon of salt and the black pepper. When the aubergine mixture has cooled, add it to the eggs and mix.

To cook the kuku, put 2 tablespoons of oil into a non-stick frying pan, around 20cm to 22cm in diameter, over a medium heat. When hot, pour the egg and aubergine mixture into the pan. Reserve a tablespoon of the dill leaves, and sprinkle the rest over the top of the egg mixture. Cook until it starts to leave the sides and the centre begins to firm up but isn't completely set. This should take around 4 minutes, but it's best to use your own judgement.

Then set a plate over the top of the pan and flip the pan over so that the kuku ends up on the plate. Shuffle or slide it back into the pan to cook the other side for another couple of minutes, or until springy to the touch.

Flip back over, using the same plate technique, so that the lovely dill leaves show on the top of the omelette, and sprinkle over the rest of the dill for good measure.

(GF) (DF)

(AUBERGINES)

SALADS

In *A Historical Dictionary of Indian Food* by India's foremost authority on the subject, K. T. Achaya, an entry for 'salad' is missing. In a country where the natural geography and soil have influenced so many different culinary styles and where the fresh produce is magnificent (and the weather relentlessly hot much of the year round), it seems a curious and glaring omission. But with a history of poor-quality water in India, it's no surprise that the country's cuisine has been built around the idea that everything has to be cooked thoroughly in order to eliminate any potential harmful bacteria. Over centuries, this has manifested itself in the cultural mindset that uncooked food is bad for you. When I cook vegetable dishes for my grandma, she'll often wrinkle her nose at me and tell me that they are *kacha paka*, which means only 'half cooked' – whereas to me, they are perfectly tender.

There is one salad every Indian knows the name of, however: kachumbar. It can be found throughout India, and is often a bright little chopped dish of cucumber, tomatoes, green chillies and lime, served alongside the daily dal, rice and subji. But more often than not, an Indian salad is still a restrained and undressed garnish of sliced carrots or lettuce, onions or radishes, making an apologetic appearance next to a dazzling curry, kebab or biryani.

Yet things are changing, but slowly. With the well-documented emergence of India's middle class aspiring to eat new, healthy dishes and quality produce, salads are gaining in popularity. While we wait for the cuisine to evolve, you will find in this chapter my imaginings of what Indian salads might look like.

CAULIFLOWER + POMEGRANATE CHAAT

(gobhi anaar chaat)

Soft, charred, creamy, crunchy, sweet and sour. Good for lunch with hot bread, or as a side to dal or chicken. Chaat masala is a spice blend made with dried sour mango powder, pomegranate seeds and ground ginger, and gives food real zing and perkiness. You can make your own (see page 287) or buy it in Asian grocery shops or online (see page 292 for suppliers).

Serves 4 as a side

1 medium cauliflower
  (about 650g)
rapeseed oil
1 x 400g tin of
  chickpeas, drained
½ a cucumber
seeds of ½ a pomegranate (see
  page 289 for how to deseed)
20g fresh coriander
1⅓ tablespoons chaat masala
  (plus extra to serve)
juice of ½ a lime
½ teaspoon salt

Break the cauliflower down into small florets using your fingers so that each one is around 1.5 to 2cm across.

Put 2mm of oil into a wide-bottomed frying pan over a high heat. Once hot, throw in the cauliflower florets and aim to have most touching the bottom of the pan so that they fry rather than steam. Cook for 8 to 10 minutes, until they are tender and charred in places, stirring every now and then. Then throw in the chickpeas and cook for another couple of minutes. Remove to a plate to cool a little, using a slotted spoon.

In the meantime, halve the cucumber lengthways and scoop out the seeds using a teaspoon, then finely slice it and transfer to a serving bowl along with the pomegranate seeds. Finely chop the coriander and add to the bowl.

Finally, add the cauliflower and chickpeas, along with the chaat masala, lime juice, salt and a tablespoon of oil. Mix together using clean hands. Sprinkle over another pinch of chaat masala just before serving.

GF DF VE

RADISH, RED ONION + POMEGRANATE SALAD

(mooli, pyaz aur anaar ka salad)

A smart and seductive salad. Marinating the red onion for an hour or so in the smashed pomegranate and lime juice takes away its punch, leaving behind fresh, bitter-sweet and peppery flavours. Perfect with a dense, buttery rice or a smoky lamb kebab, if you're that way inclined.

Serves 4 to 6 as a side

seeds of ½ a pomegranate (see
    page 289 for how to deseed)
2 tablespoons lime juice
2 teaspoons sugar
½ teaspoon salt (or to taste)
3 tablespoons rapeseed oil
a pinch of chilli powder
½ a red onion, very thinly sliced
300g mooli
200g radishes

First make the dressing. Put the pomegranate seeds into a large bowl and crush them with your (scrupulously clean) hands until they become very juicy, then add the lime juice, sugar, salt, oil and chilli powder. Mix and taste, adjusting it as you wish (you might need a little extra sugar if your pomegranate is sour). Add the red onion and leave to marinate for an hour.

Peel the mooli with a vegetable peeler and slice as thinly as you can. Wash the radishes, top and tail them, and slice thinly.

Add the radish and mooli slices to the dressing, mix well, then place on a shallow dish or rimmed platter.

FRESH MATAR PANEER

This is an update of an ageing rock star of Indian dishes – matar paneer, or paneer and pea curry. I've kept the vegetables crisp and tender so they don't surrender to mushiness: the result is a younger, edgier new kid on the block with a bit more attitude.

Serves 4 as a main course

rapeseed oil
550g hard paneer, cut
    into 1.5cm cubes
6 cloves of garlic, crushed
400g ripe plum
    tomatoes, chopped
1¼ teaspoons salt
½ teaspoon ground black pepper
1 teaspoon ground cumin
1 teaspoon chilli powder
⅓ teaspoon ground turmeric
200g green beans, topped
    and tailed
200g mangetout
200g peas (fresh or defrosted)
optional: 1 red chilli, finely sliced

Put a couple of tablespoons of oil into a frying pan over a medium heat. When hot, add the paneer and fry for around 4 minutes, until golden and crisp, turning every minute or so. Transfer the paneer to a plate using a slotted spoon.

To make the sauce, put another tablespoon of oil into the pan and, when warm, add the garlic. Stir-fry for a couple of minutes, then add the tomatoes. Cook for around 6 minutes, until the tomatoes are just starting to become jammy, then add the salt, black pepper, cumin, chilli powder and turmeric. Stir to mix, cook for another minute, then take off the heat.

Bring a pan of water to the boil. When boiling, add the beans, cook for 2 minutes, then add the mangetout. Cook for another 2 minutes, pop the peas in for a final minute, then quickly drain, allowing the veg to dry off properly in their own steam.

Heat up the sauce and add the paneer to the pan. When both are hot, add the vegetables and stir to mix. Sprinkle over the sliced red chilli.

Serve with fresh hot chapattis (see page 288) or rice, and some plain yoghurt.

PANEER, MANGO + TAMARIND SALAD

(aam, paneer aur imli ka salad)

You need hard, semi-ripe mangoes for this, as they tend to have a good balance between sweetness and acidity. They don't have to be Indian – the green Brazilian mangoes available all year round work really well. You can eat this salad by itself or with some bread, like the naan on page 220.

NOTE: As tamarind paste varies from brand to brand, add it gradually until it tastes good to you.

Serves 2 as a main course
or 4 as a side

4 tablespoons rapeseed oil
3 banana shallots, thinly sliced
450g hard paneer, cut into
   1.5cm cubes
2 teaspoons tamarind paste
salt
2 large semi-ripe mangoes
120g mixed salad leaves (e.g. baby
   spinach and lamb's lettuce)
15g fresh mint leaves,
   finely chopped
20g fresh coriander, finely chopped
1 green finger chilli, chopped
2cm ginger, peeled and chopped
3 tablespoons lime juice
1 tablespoon honey

Put 2 tablespoons of the oil into a frying pan over a medium heat and, when hot, add the shallots. Stir-fry the shallots until softened, then add the paneer.

Fry the paneer for around 4 minutes, until golden and crisp, turning every minute or so, then add the tamarind paste and ¾ teaspoon of salt. Stir-fry for a minute or two, then take off the heat.

Peel each mango with a vegetable peeler, then slice off both 'cheeks' of the mango as close to the stone as possible. Slice off the remaining sides. Cut the mango into wedges around 1cm at the thick end and put into a bowl, along with the mixed leaves, mint and coriander.

Next make the dressing. If you have a pestle and mortar, bash the green chilli and ginger together until it forms a smooth paste. If not, very finely chop both ingredients. Mix together with the lime juice, honey, ¼ teaspoon of salt and the remaining oil, then taste and adjust as you see fit.

Add the paneer mixture and dressing to the salad bowl, and mix together just before serving.

TERESA'S MANGO SALAD

(teresa ki aam salad)

When my friend Teresa made this for a party, I immediately frogmarched her straight down to the local Budgens so she could re-create it. (Sorry, Teresa.) Both this salad and Teresa are from the Seychelles, but the salad is actually Indian in origin. It's very hot and sweet, more like a condiment, so a little will go a long way. The key is the type of mango you use. They don't have to be Indian, but they do have to be semi-ripe, by which I mean hard with just the slightest amount of give when you prod them. The salad will taste better the longer you leave the mango to marinate. A couple of hours would be perfect.

It works nicely with leafy greens and coconut-based dishes like the Keralan vegetable istoo (see page 89) or fresh coconut rice (page 195).

Serves **4 as a side**

2 large semi-ripe mangoes
1 small red onion
3–4 red bird's-eye chillies,
   finely chopped
1 teaspoon salt
a grind of the pepper mill
3 tablespoons lime juice
1–2 tablespoons sugar

Using a vegetable peeler, peel the mangoes, then shave the mangoes top to bottom to create long, thin ribbons. Put them into a serving bowl.

Slice the red onion into thin half-moons and add to the bowl, along with the chillies, salt, pepper and lime juice. Add the sugar little by little – you might not need so much if your mangoes are already sweet.

Mix everything together thoroughly, and leave in the fridge for a couple of hours before serving.

  (VE)

HOT GREEN BEAN, CASHEW + COCONUT SALAD

(h a r e e p h a l e e s a l a d)

A salad greater than the sum of its parts that will dominate the dinner table delightfully. Works well with rice and sambhar (see page 173), and with beetroot shami kebabs too (page 25).

NOTE: As tamarind paste varies from brand to brand, add it gradually until it tastes good to you.

Serves 4 as a side

40g desiccated or fresh
   grated coconut
2 tablespoons rapeseed oil
½ teaspoon black mustard seeds
4 banana shallots, sliced
150g unsalted cashews
700g green beans, topped
   and tailed
1½ teaspoons tamarind paste
1 cayenne or slim red chilli
¾ teaspoon salt

Put a large pan of water on to boil.

Next, put a frying pan over a low to medium heat and, when hot, add the coconut. Stir-fry for a couple of minutes until toasted and golden, keeping a (very) watchful eye on it so that it doesn't burn, then tip on to a plate and leave to one side.

Put the oil into the same pan over a medium heat and, when hot, add the mustard seeds. When the seeds pop, add the shallots and fry for around 8 minutes, until they are soft and browning. Add the cashews, fry until golden, then take off the heat.

Meanwhile, put the beans into the pan of boiling water and cook for 4 minutes, or until tender (not too chewy but still nice and crisp to bite into), then drain and leave to dry.

Put the shallots and cashews back over a high heat and add the beans, tamarind, chilli and salt. Once everything is sizzling, toss through most of the coconut. Check for seasoning, then take off the heat and serve immediately, scattering the rest of the coconut over the top.

(SALADS)

FENNEL + APPLE CHAAT
WITH CARAMELIZED ALMONDS

(seb aur saunf ka chaat)

This crisp and clean bunch of ingredients, mixed with some warming sweet spices, works together as tightly as the rhythm section of James Brown's funk band.

Serves **4 as a side**

1 teaspoon fennel seeds
5 tablespoons rapeseed oil
100g flaked almonds
1 teaspoon ground ginger
2 tablespoons honey
salt
1 lemon, plus 2 tablespoons
    lemon juice
2 medium bulbs of fennel
3 Braeburn apples
½ a cucumber
10g fresh mint leaves,
    finely chopped
1¼ teaspoons garam masala

Grab a pestle and mortar, and bash the fennel seeds until they're coarsely ground. Next, put a couple of tablespoons of oil into a frying pan over a medium heat. When hot, add the almonds, stir-fry for a couple of minutes until they turn pale gold, then add the ground fennel seeds, ginger, honey and ⅓ teaspoon of salt. Stir-fry for another minute until caramelized. Carefully tip on to a plate and leave to cool.

To make the salad, fill a big bowl with cold water. Cut the lemon in half, squeeze the juice into the water, then chuck in the lemon halves, to stop the fennel and apple discolouring. Very finely slice (or shave on a mandolin) the fennel and put it into the lemony water. Slice the apples thinly and add them to the bowl. Cut the cucumber in half lengthways, scoop out the seeds with a teaspoon, then slice it thinly and keep to one side.

Drain the fennel and apple really well, discard the lemon halves, and put the mixture into a serving bowl along with the cucumber and mint. To make the dressing, mix together 3 tablespoons of oil with the 2 tablespoons of lemon juice, garam masala and ½ teaspoon of salt.

Crumble the caramelized almonds into the salad and pour over the dressing just before serving. Toss together using your hands or a pair of tongs, then serve.

(SALADS)   GF DF

TOMATO + CHICKPEA SALAD WITH A LIME TARKA

(tamatar chana salad)

Tarka is a technique used in Indian cooking which involves frying spices (or herbs, nuts or chillies) in oil or ghee to add flavour. Think of it as a sort of hot, spiced dressing. I've used lime and cumin together here, which really lifts all the other ingredients and takes this salad to a whole new level.

I love to eat this salad warm and in the summer when the cherry tomatoes are at their best. And I resisted mentioning anything otter-related at all. Until just now.

Serves 4 to 6 as a side

rapeseed oil
1 x 400g tin of chickpeas, drained
500g ripe baby plum tomatoes,
   quartered
6 spring onions, finely sliced
2 tablespoons ghee or butter
1 teaspoon cumin seeds,
   roughly ground
1½ green finger chillies,
   finely chopped
½ teaspoon ground black pepper
1¼ teaspoons salt
70g (or a large handful)
   unsalted cashews
juice of 1 lime
40g fresh coriander, finely chopped

Put a tablespoon of oil into a frying pan over a medium heat and, when hot, add the chickpeas. Stir-fry for a few minutes until the chickpeas are crispy, then add the tomatoes and spring onions. Stir-fry briefly to warm through, then transfer to a serving bowl.

To make the tarka, heat the ghee and 1 tablespoon of oil in a pan. When it's melted, add the ground cumin seeds, green chillies, black pepper, salt and cashews. Mix well, then fry until the cashews are golden brown, stirring occasionally. Add the lime juice, stir again, and take off the heat.

To serve, pour the tarka over the salad. Stir to mix, then add the fresh coriander and mix again.

(SALADS)

GF

SPROUTING KACHUMBAR

Turning dull, hard seeds into crunchy, fresh food using just water feels like nothing short of a miracle in a 'Jack and the Beanstalk' way. Of course, you don't need to sprout your own, as supermarkets, health food shops and Asian supermarkets have already done that for you. But if you're itching to give it a go, then turn to page 289 for instructions on how to sprout like a pro. Sprouting changes a pulse's nutritional profile: by kick-starting the whole germination process, the seed quadruples in nutrients, like potassium, protein and B vitamins, making it extraordinarily good for you.

When mixed with other companions like tomatoes, spring onions, ginger and a lively mustard dressing, sprouts make a fantastically crunchy and zingy salad, excellent with any sort of dal, rice, curry or bread.

Serves **6 as a side**

250g ripe baby plum tomatoes
200g radishes
8 spring onions
½ a cucumber
40g fresh coriander
2cm ginger, peeled
250g sprouted mung beans or
   mixed pulses

FOR THE DRESSING
2 tablespoons wholegrain mustard
1 teaspoon salt
1 teaspoon sugar
2 tablespoons rapeseed oil
juice of ½ a lemon

Chop, chop, chop all the vegetables: into tiny dice for the tomatoes; into fine slices for the radishes and spring onions (don't forget to top and tail them); then halve the cucumber lengthways, scoop the seeds out with a teaspoon and finely dice this too. Finely slice the coriander, and cut the ginger into tiny dice. Throw all the chopped vegetables and herbs into a serving bowl with the sprouted beans.

In a small bowl, whisk together the mustard, salt, sugar, oil and lemon juice and drizzle all over your salad. Boom.

LEAVES, HERBS + CURDS

Serves **4** as a side

1.5cm ginger, peeled and chopped
½ a green finger chilli
3 tablespoons rapeseed oil
2 tablespoons lemon juice
⅓ teaspoon ground cumin
⅓ teaspoon salt
¼ teaspoon ground black pepper
20g fresh coriander, chopped
20g fresh mint leaves, chopped
20g fresh dill leaves, chopped
120g mixed leaves (e.g. lamb's
   lettuce, baby chard and spinach)
50g walnuts, chopped
80g curd cheese, or cream cheese
   like Philadelphia

First make the dressing. Use a pestle and mortar to pound the ginger and green chilli until they disintegrate. Add the oil, lemon juice, cumin, salt and black pepper, and mix well.

Place the herbs and leaves in a serving bowl, scatter over the walnuts and dot teaspoon-sized balls of cheese around the salad. Just before serving, toss through the dressing.

HILL STATION SALAD

In the heat of summer, the Darjeeling hills are a great shelter from the blistering temperatures of Kolkata. But the journey from Kolkata to Darjeeling is turbulent and long, and all I ever want when I arrive (aside from a medicinal gin and tonic) is a bath and the freshest, most cooling salad I can think of. This is that salad.

Serves 6 as a side

1 medium bulb of fennel
1 medium red onion
3 mixed peppers (red,
   yellow and orange)
½ a cucumber
10g fresh coriander
1 teaspoon salt
1 teaspoon nigella seeds
   (plus extra to serve)
20g fresh mint leaves
½–1 green finger chilli
100ml Greek yoghurt
2 tablespoons lemon juice
1 teaspoon sugar (or to taste)

Remove and discard the tough outer leaves of the fennel, top and tail it, then cut off the fronds, reserving them for later. Chop the fennel bulb, red onion and peppers into 1cm dice (the smaller the better), and place in a serving bowl. Halve the cucumber lengthways, remove the seeds with a teaspoon, then chop it into 1cm dice and add to the bowl. Finely chop the coriander and add to the bowl, along with the salt and nigella seeds.

Next, make the dressing. Chop the mint and green chilli as finely as you can, put into a small bowl and mix well. Add the yoghurt, lemon juice and sugar, mix together and taste. There should be a good balance between the heat, sweetness, saltiness and lemoniness, so adjust if need be.

Pour the dressing over the salad just before serving and mix well. Sprinkle over the fennel fronds, and a few more nigella seeds for good measure.

PRESENTATION SKILLS

Thankfully we've all moved on from the 1980s and there's no longer a need to crinkle-cut eggs, julienne everything and carve flowers out of radishes, but that's not to say that we shouldn't think about food presentation. We also eat with our eyes, feasting on colours and textures, but so often some of the most delicious curries in the world can look surprisingly ugly. While I will never be an advocate of painting plates with brushstroked sauces, there are a few tips worth having up your sleeve when it comes to making Indian food look beautiful. In choosing these, think about which colours, textures and flavours will go well with what you're cooking.

CURRIES + DALS

Things in sauce can look muddy, but chopped coriander doesn't need to be the only answer. One or a combination of these can work really nicely.

YOGHURT OR CREAM

A drizzle or dollop is always useful. Or even a Jackson Pollock splatter. Sometimes I'll put curries into individual bowls, add a dollop of yoghurt on the side, and scatter with some nuts or finely chopped herbs.

FRIED SHALLOTS OR ONIONS

Halve an onion or two, or a handful of shallots, and cut into thin half-moons. Warm a slick of oil in a pan over a medium to low heat, and throw the onions in. Stir every now and then for 20 minutes or so, until they become dark brown and crispy. Then scoop out, drain, and throw a small mound in the middle of your curry.

A QUICK HERB CHUTNEY

Chop a large handful of coriander – stems and leaves – as finely as you can and place in a bowl. Add ½ a finely chopped green chilli, pour in a little oil and, little by little, season with salt and lemon juice until it tastes just right.

FRIED CHICKPEAS

Crisp chickpeas can add a lovely texture. Put a couple of tablespoons of oil into a frying pan over a medium heat. When hot, throw in a can of drained chickpeas and stir-fry until the skins turn crisp, then transfer to a bowl and sprinkle over salt and ground cumin or black pepper, or chaat masala, or garam masala, little by little, until you think you've got enough flavour.

GOLDEN COCONUT FLAKES

Crisp golden coconut crescents can look on point. To toast them, add a teaspoon of oil to a frying pan over a medium heat and add a handful. Stir-fry for a minute, watch like a hawk, and tip out when they start to colour.

RICE

You can do no harm by scattering spices, nuts, herbs or fruit over rice, or tangling fried onions into it.

CRUSHED CUMIN SEEDS

The quickest addition to rice is to crush cumin seeds in a pestle and mortar until you have a nice combination of seeds and powder, then sprinkle it over the rice, starting in the centre. If you've got time, toast the cumin in a dry frying pan for a few minutes until it turns a mahogany colour – it will give it a lovely warm flavour.

PAN-FRIED CASHEWS, PISTACHIOS, PEANUTS OR FLAKED ALMONDS

I love the golden bronze of pan-fried nuts cheekily peeking out of some snow-white rice. Heat a couple of teaspoons of oil in a frying pan and add the nuts when hot, stir-fry for a minute or so until they develop a lovely colour, then tip out of the pan so they stop cooking.

BLACKENED RAISINS

These are a recent favourite. Throw a handful of raisins into a hot pan with a drop of oil, stir-fry until they puff up into round balls, then scatter over the rice. They will be deliciously chewy and crunchy.

PUDDINGS

CRUSHED PISTACHIOS

You can grind a handful of pistachios with a pestle and mortar or food processor to a coarse texture. Or blitz them to a dust, which I love to do with a little jaggery to sprinkle over dairy desserts, fruit, kulfi and lassis.

POMEGRANATES

There is nothing a few beautiful pomegranate jewels can't make look better. For how to deseed a pomegranate, turn to page 289.

CRUMBLED ROSE PETALS

A few dried crumbled petals can make a dessert look pretty, especially when combined with a few berries or pomegranate kernels or even chopped pistachios. If you have your own (unsprayed) rose petals, you can make sugared petals by brushing both sides with egg white, then coating in caster sugar and leaving to dry for a few hours or overnight. They'll keep in a plastic container for a few weeks.

EGGS + CHEESE

In the ancient Hindu text *Chandogya Upanishad*, the cracking of an egg marked the start of the universe. The shell became the mountains, the white became the oceans and the yolk the sun.

The egg has been eulogized for thousands of years in India, and is still a major source of protein in the Indian diet today. As an egg-o-phile, I need no convincing of its merits. No other ingredient to me seems as complete – as nutritionally dense, as satisfying by itself or even as full of possibility to become so many things.

In India, it is eaten throughout the day in a dazzling array of dishes, from spiced scrambled eggs to dinner-time curries and elaborate omelettes fit for a king.

The treatment of eggs is often bound up in rules, but I only have one: buy eggs that have come from happy, free-range chickens.

When it comes to cheese, Indians have eyes for just one: paneer. This is probably because India is a nation of home cooks and this is the simplest cheese in the world to make (see page 286), using just two ingredients: milk and lemon juice. In addition, more complicated cheeses are traditionally made with rennet, an ingredient found in the stomachs of cows, goats or sheep which can only be extracted after their slaughter, making them unsuitable for Hindu vegetarians.

Like eggs, paneer can take on different personalities. When made at home, it is soft and crumbles easily, with a similar texture to feta and a flavour like ricotta. When you buy paneer in the shops, it comes in two forms: either crumbly, like the home-made version, or, more commonly, hard and in blocks, with a texture more like halloumi.

Neither is salted, flavoured or matured in the same way as British Cheddars or blue cheeses; instead, they are best treated as ingredients. The soft crumbly version is delicate, and great with fresh flavours like peas, lemon and cumin. The harder one is excellent to sizzle in a pan or on a griddle or barbecue until the edges crisp and char and the inside melts. You can either marinate it beforehand or throw it into a sauce afterwards.

A final note to vegans (if you're still reading): the majority of the recipes in this section can become vegan if you substitute oil for ghee, and swap the eggs or paneer for tofu, which has a similar texture to hard paneer and takes flavour really well.

EGGS KEJRIWAL

This is a bona fide Mumbai classic, named after the Mr Kejriwal who used to order it every day for breakfast at the Willingdon Club, thirty years ago. After years of persistence, they finally put it on the menu and millions of Mumbaikers have enjoyed it ever since.

Traditionally, this recipe is made using a basic Cheddar, but Lincolnshire Poacher is a game-changer for the Kejriwal. Its sweet, nutty and fruity flavour is perfect with the fresh heat of the chilli. If you can't find it, though, a good mature Cheddar will be absolutely fine.

Serves 2 for breakfast

4 door-stopper slices of
  good bread
Colman's mustard
1–2 green finger chillies, sliced
  paper thin
200g Lincolnshire Poacher or
  mature Cheddar, grated
1 tablespoon unsalted butter
4 medium eggs
salt and ground black pepper

Preheat the grill to a medium to high heat.

Lightly toast the bread in a toaster or put a frying pan over a medium heat and pan-fry each side for a minute or two. Spread each slice with a thin layer of mustard.

Mix three-quarters of the chilli into the cheese and layer over the toast, then pop under the grill until the cheese starts to blister and brown. Transfer to plates when ready.

In the meantime, melt the butter in a frying pan over a medium heat and fry the eggs until the whites have set but the yolks are still runny. Place on the cheese toasts.

Sprinkle a little salt over the top, along with a decent amount of black pepper and the remaining chilli, and serve immediately.

AKOORI

Everyone has their own way of doing scrambled eggs. Akoori is the Parsi way. The Parsis are Iranians who, fleeing persecution, arrived in India in AD 936. Their mantra is 'good thoughts, good words and good deeds', but they might as well tag on 'good eggs' because they know a thing or two about them.

This dish has been a Sunday-morning family favourite for years. It's especially loved by Dad, as the short list of store-cupboard ingredients means he never has to pop out to grab anything.

Serves 4 for breakfast

1 teaspoon cumin seeds
8 medium eggs
30g unsalted butter
2 red onions, finely chopped
2 ripe tomatoes, chopped
1½ green finger chillies, finely chopped
½ teaspoon salt
½ teaspoon ground black pepper
2 tablespoons finely chopped fresh coriander

Coarsely crush the cumin seeds in a pestle and mortar and leave to one side. Crack the eggs into a bowl and lightly beat with a fork, then leave to one side too.

Next, put the butter into a frying pan over a medium heat. When melted, add the crushed cumin and the red onions and fry for 12 to 15 minutes, until the onions are soft, golden and caramelized. Then add the tomatoes, green chillies, salt and black pepper.

Toss the tomatoes around for 30 seconds to a minute, then turn the heat to low and pour in the eggs. Keep stirring continuously. Don't worry if it takes a while to cook them: they will be all the creamier for it. When the eggs start to clump but are still soft, take off the heat and stir through the chopped coriander.

Serve with buttered toast and chai.

(EGGS + CHEESE)

GF

BENGALI-IN-THE-CUPBOARD EGG CURRY

(dimer johl)

I'd love to tell you a story about how I once found a man from Bengal hiding in a cupboard, but sadly that isn't true. This is a classic Bengali curry, and rather happily this dish can probably be made using ingredients from your store cupboard.

NOTE: The bay leaves in this curry are Indian bay leaves, which have a flavour similar to cinnamon. They are very different from European bay leaves, so if you can't find them, leave them out.

Serves 4 as a main course

4 cm ginger, peeled and
   chopped
5 cloves of garlic, chopped
salt
3 tablespoons rapeseed oil
2 red onions, finely diced
2 Indian bay leaves
500g tomato passata
1 teaspoon chilli powder
½ teaspoon ground cinnamon
1½ teaspoons ground cumin
1½ teaspoons garam masala
½ teaspoon ground turmeric
½ teaspoon sugar
8 eggs

Use a pestle and mortar to grind the ginger and garlic to a paste with ¼ teaspoon of salt, and leave to one side.

Put the oil into a large saucepan over a medium heat and, when hot, add the red onions and bay leaves. Fry for 10 minutes, until the onions are soft and starting to brown, then add the ginger and garlic paste. Stir to mix, fry for a few minutes, then add the passata.

Leave to cook for around 10 minutes, or until the tomatoes have thickened nicely. Then add the chilli powder, cinnamon, cumin, garam masala, turmeric, 1 teaspoon of salt and the sugar, and cook for a further 10 minutes.

In the meantime, boil the eggs. Put them into a deep-sided pan and fill with enough water to submerge them. Bring the water to the boil, then turn it down to a simmer and cook for 6 minutes for a squidgy yolk. Run the eggs under a cold tap for a minute and peel.

Halve the eggs and fold them into the curry, then serve immediately with big, delicious naan breads or some rice.

PARK STREET KATI ROLLS

Kolkata is a magical city. The Hooghly River surges through the middle, and tropical birds fly in and out of beautiful crumbling buildings and among the banyan trees. Men in velvet jackets discuss politics in underground bars, while hundreds of boys fling cricket balls in the central park. But these aren't the only reasons why you should visit. On Park Street, there is a man who serves the best kati rolls. A kati roll is made using an egg-fried paratha wrapped around sweet peppers and paneer, with a little green chilli chutney to finish. This is my attempt to re-create the best thing to have come out of Kolkata since Mother Teresa.

NOTE: You will need a blender to make the chilli chutney in this recipe.

Makes 4 rolls (enough for
   2 to 4 people for lunch)

80g fresh coriander,
   roughly chopped
2 tablespoons lemon juice
salt
rapeseed oil
2 green finger chillies, chopped
2 medium eggs
225g hard paneer, cut into
   8cm x 1cm strips
1 red onion, sliced
3 mixed peppers (red and
   yellow), sliced
1 teaspoon chilli powder
1 teaspoon ground coriander
1 teaspoon ground cumin
4 parathas or wraps

First make the chutney. Put the fresh coriander, lemon juice, ½ teaspoon of salt, 4 tablespoons of oil and the green chillies into a blender along with 4 tablespoons of water and whizz together.

Next, crack the eggs into a small bowl and lightly beat with a fork. Heat a tablespoon of oil in a frying pan and, when hot, add the paneer strips. Fry for 3 to 4 minutes, until brown and crispy, turning frequently, then transfer to a plate.

Put another tablespoon of oil into the same pan and, when hot, add the onion and peppers. Cook for 8 to 10 minutes, until starting to soften, then add the chilli powder, ground coriander, cumin and ¾ teaspoon of salt. Stir, then add the fried paneer. Cook for a minute, then take off the heat and cover to keep warm.

To cook the egg parathas or wraps, put a large frying pan over a medium heat. When hot, place a paratha in the pan for 30 seconds, then flip, and pour a quarter of the egg mixture over the top. Wait for a minute for the egg to set, then flip again. Let it cook for 30 seconds – the egg will start to puff up – then transfer to a plate.

Place a quarter of the paneer and pepper mixture into the centre, add a dollop of chutney and roll up. Repeat with the other parathas and eat while still hot. To keep them warm, you can wrap each one tightly in foil, like a baby in a blanket.

EGG HOPPERS WITH ONION SAMBOL

This is Sri Lanka's favourite breakfast: lacy rice crêpes fashioned into bowls, with an egg nestling in the middle, topped with sweet spicy onion sambol and zingy lime juice. It's a heavenly combination of flavours. Traditionally, in Sri Lanka, hoppers are made by fermenting rice overnight, but I've created this variation based on an old Charmaine Solomon recipe in which you just need to rest the batter for an hour. The bowl shape comes from a special 'hopper pan', but a small non-stick omelette pan with a lid will work well in its place.

Makes 8 hoppers (enough for 4 people for breakfast)

FOR THE EGG HOPPERS
2 teaspoons yeast
1½ teaspoons sugar
110g self-raising flour
170g rice flour
1 teaspoon salt
380ml hand-hot water
rapeseed oil
8 medium eggs
1 lime, cut into 8 wedges
a handful of fresh
   coriander leaves

FOR THE ONION SAMBOL
4 cardamom pods
4 tablespoons rapeseed oil
4 whole cloves
4cm cinnamon stick
500g red onions, finely sliced
1 teaspoon salt
1½ teaspoons chilli powder
2 teaspoons sugar

To make the hoppers, place the yeast, sugar, flours and salt in a large bowl and whisk together to combine. Add the water and whisk well until you have a smooth consistency. Place the bowl in a warm spot (like an airing cupboard, or slightly warm oven) for 15 minutes, or until the mixture is full of bubbles. It's then ready to go.

Next, make the onion sambol. Bash the cardamom pods with a pestle and mortar until cracked. Heat the oil in a large frying pan and, when hot, add the cloves, cardamom and cinnamon stick. When you can smell the spices, add the red onions, salt and chilli powder and cook over a low to medium heat for 30 to 40 minutes, stirring occasionally to ensure the onions don't burn. At the end, stir in the sugar and cook until dissolved. Check the seasoning and take off the heat.

To cook the hoppers, take either a hopper pan or a small lidded non-stick frying pan and rub the inside with some oil-dipped kitchen paper. Put it over a low to medium heat. When hot, whisk the bubbly batter and pour a ladleful into the pan. Holding the pan by the handle(s), quickly twist it so the batter coats the bottom and all the way around the sides. Cook for a minute until the batter has set, then crack an egg into the middle and cover with the lid. Cook for a further 3 to 4 minutes, until the whites of the egg are set and the hopper batter has left the sides of the pan, then slide or gently lever on to a plate. The hopper should be crisp, and golden on the outside, and the egg yolk runny in the middle. Repeat, adjusting your timings if need be.

Top the hopper with a spoonful of onion sambol (remove any spices you don't want to bite into), a wedge of lime and some coriander, and eat straight away.

PANEER KEBABS WITH MINT + CORIANDER

(hara paneer tikka)

Paneer is often in need of something to sharpen up its smooth creaminess and give it a kick in the right direction. In this case, the mint and coriander marinade does a fabulous job.

NOTE: You will need a blender for this recipe.

Makes 6 to 8 skewers
(enough for 4 people)

rapeseed oil
2 tablespoons chickpea
(gram) flour
60g fresh coriander
30g fresh mint leaves
100ml Greek yoghurt
4 cloves of garlic
2 green finger chillies
1⅓ teaspoons salt
2 tablespoons lemon juice
600g hard paneer, cut into
3cm cubes
2 green or yellow peppers,
cut into 3cm pieces

Preheat the oven to 220°C/425°F/gas 7 and line an oven tray with lightly oiled foil. If you're using wooden skewers, soak them in a bowl of cold water and leave to one side.

Put 2 tablespoons of oil into a frying pan over a medium heat and, when hot, add the chickpea flour. Fry the flour for a couple of minutes, until it develops a nutty smell and turns the shade of almond skin, then take off the heat.

Put the coriander, mint leaves, yoghurt, garlic, green chillies, salt and lemon juice into a blender and whizz to a fine paste. Combine with the chickpea flour paste and mix well. Coat the paneer cubes in the mixture, and marinate for at least 15 minutes and up to a couple of hours.

When you're ready to cook, thread the paneer and pepper pieces alternately on to the skewers. Place the skewers on the oven tray and bake for 12 to 15 minutes, turning halfway. The paneer should be charring and crisp on the edges and super-soft inside.

Serve with cucumber and mint raita (see page 247), naan bread and a fresh salad or rice.

STICKY MANGO PANEER SKEWERS

(aam ki chutney wala paneer)

Jim Pizer is more Indian than a lot of Indians I know. While growing up he was in and out of his Indian friends' houses in Birmingham, eating their mums' home cooking, and was so disappointed with the state of Indian food in restaurants in the UK that he decided to set up his own, the Thali Café in Bristol. It did so well that, ten years later, one restaurant has grown into five.

This is one of the most popular dishes on the menu and always has been. Although you might not find it on menus in India, it's one of the finest ways to eat paneer that I know.

Makes **6 to 8 kebabs**
    (enough for 4 people)

3 tablespoons rapeseed oil
2 tablespoons chickpea
    (gram) flour
600g hard paneer, cut into
    3cm cubes
4cm ginger, peeled and grated
6 cloves of garlic, crushed
1¼ teaspoons chilli powder
2 tablespoons mango chutney
1½ teaspoons ground
    black pepper
1¼ teaspoons salt
½ teaspoon ground turmeric
2 tablespoons tomato puree
2 tablespoons chopped
    fresh coriander
1½ red peppers, cut into
    3cm chunks

Put the oil into a small pan over a medium heat. When hot, add the chickpea flour and stir into the oil. Reduce the heat to low and stir until the oil is absorbed and you have a paste. Don't allow it to burn, but aim for a nutty brown colour – this is where the deeply savoury flavour of the marinade comes from. Allow the paste to cool for 3 minutes.

Put the chickpea flour mixture into a bowl with the paneer and all the other ingredients apart from the red pepper. Mix well and leave to marinate for at least 15 minutes (the longer the better). If you're using wooden skewers, soak them in a bowl of cold water and leave to one side.

When you're ready to cook, thread the paneer pieces alternately with the red pepper on to the skewers. Meanwhile, heat up a griddle pan, frying pan or barbecue. Cook the kebabs for around 8 minutes, turning them every couple of minutes, until they are lovely and chargrilled on each side.

Serve immediately, with naan bread or rice, cucumber and mint raita (see page 247) and a salad, like the hill station salad on page 143.

GF

PANEER STUFFED ROMANO PEPPERS

(paneer bhari mirchi)

I'm a child of the eighties – no one can stop me from stuffing peppers. These make for a beautiful starter alongside simply dressed leaves, and you can, if you want, stuff the peppers and refrigerate them, then roast them when you want to eat them.

Serves 4 as a starter or part of a main course

4 large Romano peppers
2 tablespoons rapeseed oil
1 teaspoon cumin
   seeds, crushed
1 brown onion, finely diced
1 green finger chilli,
   very finely chopped
2cm ginger, peeled and grated
225g hard paneer, grated
1 large ripe tomato,
   finely chopped
⅓ teaspoon salt
⅓ teaspoon chilli powder
20g fresh coriander, chopped

Preheat the oven to 180°C/350°F/gas 4 and line an oven tray with baking paper or foil.

Slice open the top of a pepper, 1cm below the stem, but don't slice it off – keep it intact. Then slice down the middle of the pepper. Open it up with your hands, gently pull out the seeds and discard. Repeat with the rest of the peppers.

Put a frying pan on a medium heat. When hot, add the oil and the crushed cumin seeds and stir-fry for 30 seconds, then add the onion. Fry for around 8 minutes, until soft, then add the green chilli and ginger and cook for another couple of minutes. Add the paneer and tomato, cook for a further 5 minutes, or until soft, then add the salt, chilli powder and coriander. Mix well, take off the heat and allow to cool.

Divide the mixture into four and stuff each pepper using a spoon or clean fingers. Press the pepper closed, lay on the oven tray, then bake for 20 minutes, or until the peppers are soft and slightly charred in places.

PANEER BUTTER MASALA

Hindus consider cows and all their milky produce – cream, butter and cheese – sacred. I can't argue with that. Traditionally, this dish would be made with a few large slabs of golden butter, but for the sake of decency I've toned things down a bit. It's still an extravagant dish, but channel India and enjoy yourself.

Serves 4 as a main course

rapeseed oil
500g hard paneer, cut into
    2cm cubes
3 tablespoons unsalted butter
1 large brown onion,
    finely chopped
4cm ginger, peeled and grated
6 cloves of garlic, crushed
800g tomato passata
1 tablespoon kasoori methi
    (dried fenugreek leaves)
1 teaspoon ground cinnamon
¼ teaspoon ground cloves
½ teaspoon chilli powder
2 tablespoons honey
1½ teaspoons salt
250g peas (fresh or defrosted)
100ml double cream (plus
    extra to serve)
a handful of toasted
    flaked almonds

Put a tablespoon of oil into a large lidded frying pan over a medium heat and, when hot, add the cubes of paneer. Fry for a couple of minutes until golden on all sides, turning regularly, then remove to a plate.

Put the butter into the same pan over a medium heat. When hot, add the onion and fry for around 10 minutes, until translucent and turning golden. Add the ginger and garlic, stir-fry for 2 to 3 minutes, then add the passata. Cover with the lid and cook for 12 to 15 minutes, until reduced to a lovely thick sauce.

Add the fenugreek leaves, cinnamon, cloves, chilli powder, honey and salt to the pan. Stir, then add the fried paneer, cover with a lid and cook for 5 minutes, or until cooked through. Add the peas and cream and cook for a further 5 minutes.

To serve, scatter with the almonds and drizzle with a little extra cream. This curry is perfect with steamed basmati rice.

(EGGS + CHEESE)
GF

PULSES

Of all the things that happened just after *Made in India* was published, cooking my mother's 'daily dal' live on Radio 4's *Woman's Hour* with Jenni Murray was the most surreal. After which, I received a barrage of messages from people across the world who were both thrilled and surprised that you can cook dal so quickly, without first soaking the lentils. It made me realize how confusing the world of pulses can be. Most of them look the same, sitting dustily in packets with little explanation of what to do with them.

Far from being worthy or boring, pulses can be transformed into deliciousness with just a few other ingredients, they're cheap and filling, and full of protein and complex carbohydrates to boot. In India, they are the lifeblood of a country of a billion and cooked daily. You'll never be more than two metres away from a bubbling pot of dal.

In order to coax you into cooking a few unfamiliar ones, here's a quick lowdown on the pulses used in this chapter and how best to cook them. When it comes to whole pulses, it's up to you whether you choose to buy tinned or cook them from scratch. I always keep tins of chickpeas, kidney beans and black-eyed beans (in unsalted water) in my cupboard because it allows me to knock up dinner in under 30 minutes. But when I have more time, I love to cook pulses from dried because they are undeniably more voluptuous and creamy. There's not a lot of effort involved either, you just need time. I wash and soak the beans just before I go to bed, then drain, rinse and cover with fresh water in the morning and boil until tender.

When it comes to split pulses, or dal, you can only buy these in their dried form, so they need to be boiled first. There are quick-cooking dals and slow ones: each has its merits and they vary in flavour. I've given flavour notes, soaking times, cooking times and availability of all the pulses below.

Just a couple more things to note. Some people add bicarbonate of soda when soaking to soften the beans and reduce cooking times. You can add a pinch if you want to, but I've not noticed a huge difference in texture or timings. Also, never salt pulses before they have cooked, as salt toughens them; only add it after they've cooked.

KNOW YOUR PULSES

BLACK-EYED BEANS, OR LOBIA

Creamy soft beans which pick up other flavours easily and go well with tomatoes and garlic. I use them with roast pumpkin and coconut on page 169. Tinned are easily available and wonderful, but if you'd like to use dried, soak overnight and boil for 45 minutes to an 1 hour. They are done when creamy not chalky inside.

KIDNEY BEANS, OR RAJMA

More than any other pulse, I find a really noticeable difference between tinned and cooked kidney beans: the tinned can be chalky, while the cooked are impossibly creamy. Widely available and worth experimenting with. Soak overnight, bring to a boil, boil for 10 minutes, then simmer for up to an hour until tender.

RED LENTILS, OR MASOOR DAL

These are one of the most commonly available lentils, found from corner shops to supermarkets. They are the split halves of the brown lentil, and a dream to cook: no soaking and quick cooking. Just wash until the water runs clear, bring to a boil and simmer for 20 minutes. These are done when they lose their shape and start to disintegrate.

SPLIT BLACK GRAM, OR CHANA DAL

You can buy split black gram, or black chickpeas, in larger supermarkets, Asian supermarkets or online. They're worth cooking as they have a delicious sweet nutty flavour that doesn't need much spice, making them perfect in the subtle Bengali coconut dal on page 176. Soak for an hour in warm water and boil for 45 minutes.

SPLIT YELLOW MUNG BEANS, OR MOONG DAL

Mung beans are hard green little beans native to India; mung dal are the split ivory-coloured insides of the mung bean. They are available in Asian supermarkets or online, and make the most comforting buttery dal (see page 170). To cook, wash them, bring to the boil and simmer for 30 to 40 minutes. They will lose their shape when done.

SPROUTED MUNG BEANS, OR MOONG

In addition to their incredible nutritional credentials, these sprouted beans are juicy, nutty and substantial all at once. Easy to sprout (see page 289) in 48 hours with a little water, but also readily available in supermarkets. There is no need for cooking, although my mum maintains it's better for your stomach to heat them through before eating.

WHITE LENTILS, OR SPLIT URAD DAL

White lentils start life as whole black urad beans which are then skinned and split. These are very special lentils, used to make some of India's best-loved dishes, from poppadoms and dosas to idlis and lentil fritters. They have a mild, creamy flavour which develops well when fermented. To get the most out of them, it's best to soak them overnight, then grind them into a batter using a blender or food processer.

YELLOW SPLIT PIGEON PEAS, OR TOOR OR ARHAR DAL

One of India's most popular lentils, it's these that go into our Gujarati dal (see page 179). They look strikingly similar to chana dal, and are available in Asian supermarkets and online. To cook them, wash, then soak for 1 hour in warm water and simmer for another hour. Most people cook them until they disintegrate, but I like a little bite to mine. They will keep their shape until whisked, and are done when they've lost their chalkiness.

PUMPKIN, BLACK-EYED BEAN + COCONUT CURRY

(olan)

The smell of roasted pumpkin, and curry leaves sizzling in coconut oil, is enough to make anyone want to go to Kerala, which is where a variation of this dish, known as 'olan', originates. The sweet pumpkin, earthy beans and creamy coconut come together to create a gentle curry, perfect for eating in England in the autumn, when a variety of pumpkins and squashes abound.

Serves 4 as a main course

1.2kg pumpkin or squash
rapeseed oil
1 tablespoon garam masala
salt and ground black pepper
coconut or rapeseed oil
1 teaspoon mustard seeds
2 green finger chillies, slit
   lengthways
1 large onion, halved and
   thinly sliced
3 cloves of garlic, crushed
1 x 400g tin of black-eyed
   beans, drained
150g ripe tomatoes,
   cut into wedges
⅓ teaspoon ground turmeric
1 x 400ml tin of coconut milk
optional: 10 fresh curry leaves

Preheat the oven to 200°C/400°F/gas 6 and line two baking trays with foil. Cut the pumpkin in half, scoop out and discard the seeds, then cut it into crescents around 2cm at the widest part. Transfer to a big bowl, drizzle with oil, and sprinkle with the garam masala, 1 teaspoon of salt and ½ teaspoon of black pepper. Toss to coat evenly, then arrange in a single layer. Roast for 30 minutes, or until soft and tender.

Meanwhile, put 2 tablespoons of oil into a large lidded frying pan over a medium heat and, when hot, add the mustard seeds. When they pop, add the slit green chillies and the onion. Cook for 12 minutes, or until the onion is soft and golden, then add the garlic. Cook for another couple of minutes, then add the drained beans and stir to mix together. Add the tomatoes and cook for a few more minutes until soft and jammy around the edges.

Next, add the turmeric, ⅓ teaspoon of black pepper, ½ teaspoon of salt and the coconut milk. Tip the roasted pumpkin into the pan and stir to mix. Cover with the lid and leave to heat through for 5 minutes. Check for salt and chilli, adjusting if you wish, then transfer to a serving dish.

If you like, you can finish off the dish with a quick curry leaf tarka: put 2 tablespoons of oil into a small frying pan over a medium to high heat. When hot, throw in the curry leaves and let them crackle and turn translucent in the oil. Pour over the pumpkin, then serve.

This dish goes well with elephant ear naan (see page 220), tamarind and caramelized red onion rice (page 192) and some cucumber and mint raita (page 247).

MOONG DAL WITH A GARLIC + CUMIN TARKA

(moong dal tarka)

This is an unassuming but gorgeous dal and one of my favourite lentil dishes of all time. A gentle and soothing marriage of soft lentils and earthy cumin and chillies, tempered by butter, it's old-fashioned home cooking at its best: nourishing, cheap to make and comforting.

Serves 4 as part of a main course

300g moong dal
4 tablespoons ghee or unsalted butter
1½ teaspoons cumin seeds
3 banana shallots, finely sliced
2 green finger chillies, very thinly sliced
5 cloves of garlic, crushed
½ teaspoon ground turmeric
1 teaspoon garam masala
1½ teaspoons salt (or to taste)

Wash the dal until the water runs clear, then drain, place in a deep saucepan and cover with 1½ litres of water. Bring to the boil, turn down the heat, and simmer for 30 to 40 minutes, until tender.

Meanwhile, put the ghee or butter into a frying pan over a medium heat and, when hot, add the cumin seeds and shallots. Cook for around 5 minutes, then add the green chillies and garlic. Cook for another 5 minutes, or until the shallots start to brown, then add the turmeric and garam masala.

Tip into the dal and stir, then add the salt. You might need to add a little extra hot water to make the dal a bit thinner. Check the seasoning, and serve with plain basmati rice or naan bread, together with some pickle and yoghurt.

GF

BUTTERNUT SQUASH, AUBERGINE + RED LENTIL SAMBHAR

In the 1960s and '70s when English curry-house menus were first printed and laminated, South Indian food hardly got a look-in. The strange outcome of this trend has been that many lovers of Indian food have hardly tried classic South Indian dishes such as sambhar, a lentil-based vegetable stew that is eaten daily all the way from Mumbai to Bangalore. Sambhar puts vegetables front and centre and surrounds them with sharp, clean flavours like curry leaves, tamarind, tomatoes and chillies. You'll only need a little rice or bread with this, and a dollop of yoghurt, and you're away.

NOTE: As tamarind paste varies from brand to brand, add it gradually until it tastes good to you.

Serves 4 as a main course

200g red lentils
4 tablespoons rapeseed oil
¼ teaspoon fenugreek seeds
2 teaspoons coriander seeds
1½ teaspoons cumin seeds
¾ teaspoon mustard seeds
12–15 fresh curry leaves
4 banana shallots, finely sliced
250g butternut squash,
   chopped into 3cm cubes
1 medium aubergine (300g),
   chopped into 3cm cubes
4 medium ripe
   tomatoes, chopped
1¾ teaspoons salt
1½ teaspoons sugar
2 teaspoons tamarind paste
1½ teaspoons chilli powder
200g green beans, trimmed

Wash the lentils with cold water until the water runs clear, then put into a deep saucepan, cover with three times the amount of water and bring to the boil. Simmer for 25 minutes, or until soft, scooping off any foam.

Meanwhile, put 1 tablespoon of oil into a wide lidded frying pan and add the fenugreek, coriander and cumin seeds. Stir-fry for a minute, then take off the heat and grind to a coarse paste with a pestle and mortar.

Put the remaining oil into the frying pan over a medium to high heat. When hot, add the mustard seeds and curry leaves, followed closely by the shallots, and cook for around 10 minutes, until the shallots are golden. Then add the diced squash and a couple of tablespoons of water, cover with the lid and cook for 5 minutes.

Add the aubergine and another couple of tablespoons of water, cover and cook for another 5 minutes, then add the tomatoes, along with the spices you ground earlier, the salt, sugar, tamarind paste and chilli powder. Cover again and leave to cook for a further 5 minutes, until the tomatoes have broken down and the squash is tender. Add the lentils to the vegetables (or the other way around, depending on which pan is bigger), then add the green beans and enough water to make a thick, soupy texture, and cook for a final 5 minutes. Taste and adjust the salt, sugar and tamarind as you wish.

Divide the sambhar into bowls, spoon over some yoghurt, and serve with rice.

SRI LANKAN DAL WITH COCONUT + LIME KALE

This classic and soothing creamy red lentil Sri Lankan dal is offset by spiky 'mallum', or shredded greens cooked with onions, coconut and fresh lime. In Sri Lanka all sorts of nutritious greens are used to make mallum, from chrysanthemum leaves to turnip tops. I use iron-rich kale here because it works harmoniously with the coconut and lime, but feel free to play around with spinach, cabbage or whatever greens are in season.

Serves 4 as a main course

450g red lentils
3 cardamom pods
coconut oil
1 cinnamon stick
3 whole cloves
2 brown onions, thinly sliced
4 cloves of garlic, crushed
2cm ginger, peeled and grated
2 green finger chillies,
    finely sliced
⅓ teaspoon ground turmeric
250g kale
200ml tinned coconut milk
salt
½ teaspoon mustard seeds
2 tablespoons desiccated or
    fresh grated coconut
juice of 1 lime

Wash the lentils in cold water until the water runs clear, then cover in water and leave to one side. Bash the cardamom pods with a pestle and mortar until cracked.

Put 2 tablespoons of coconut oil into a deep lidded saucepan over a medium heat and, when hot, add the cardamom, cinnamon stick and cloves. Stir-fry for a minute, then add the onions. Cook for 10 minutes, until the onions are browning and soft, stirring frequently, then add the garlic, ginger and green chillies. Stir-fry for another couple of minutes, then remove a third of the mixture and leave it to one side.

Drain the lentils and add to the pan, along with the turmeric and 1 litre of hot water. Bring to the boil, then turn the heat right down and simmer for 20 to 25 minutes, until the lentils are soft and creamy. In the meantime, wash the kale and chop the leaves into 5cm strips, discarding the thicker stems. When the lentils are ready, add the coconut milk and 1½ teaspoons of salt, cook for another 5 minutes, then take off the heat. Cover to keep warm.

To make the kale mallum, put a tablespoon of coconut oil into a lidded frying pan over a medium heat and, when hot, add the mustard seeds. When they pop, put the reserved onion mixture into the pan and fry for a couple of minutes, then add the kale and desiccated coconut. Stir-fry for a minute, then add 50ml of water and put the lid on. Leave to steam for 4 minutes, then add the lime juice and ½ teaspoon of salt and stir. Put the lid back on and steam for another 2 minutes, or until the kale is soft and tender.

To serve, ladle the dal into bowls and divide the kale over the top. Serve with rice and yoghurt.

BENGALI COCONUT DAL

(cholar dal)

This is a gentle and luxurious dal, nutty from the split chickpeas, and sweet and creamy from the cinnamon, cardamom and coconut.

Serves **4 as part of a main course**

300g chana dal
4 tablespoons desiccated or fresh grated coconut
2 tablespoons mustard oil or rapeseed oil
3 cloves of garlic, finely sliced
4cm ginger, peeled and grated
2 red bird's-eye chillies, slit lengthways
3 medium ripe tomatoes, chopped
½ teaspoon ground turmeric
1 teaspoon ground cinnamon
⅓ teaspoon ground cloves
½ teaspoon ground cardamom (or finely ground seeds from 6 pods)
1¼ teaspoons salt
1 teaspoon sugar

Wash the chana dal in a few changes of cold water until the water runs clear, then soak for an hour in warm water. Put into a saucepan with twice the amount of water and boil for around 45 minutes, until soft, then leave to one side.

Put a frying pan over a medium heat and toast the coconut until just starting to brown, stirring frequently, then tip into a bowl. Put the oil, garlic, ginger and red chillies into the frying pan and stir until the garlic is starting to brown, then add the tomatoes. Cook for around 5 minutes, until the tomatoes break down into a paste.

Now add the spices, together with the salt and sugar. Stir-fry for a couple of minutes, then add the mixture to the chana dal, along with the toasted coconut, and stir well.

Taste your dal, adjusting the salt as need be, and topping up with hot water until it's at a consistency you like. Cook through over a medium heat for another 5 minutes or so to bring all the flavours together.

(PULSES)

TEMPLE TOMATO RASAM

(tamatar ki rasam)

In India, food and religion go hand in hand. Most Hindu kitchens have god figurines nestled in among the pots, pans and spices, and most temples have a lively kitchen attached. Visits to temples usually involve a meal of some kind, and one of the most common dishes served in the south is this rasam, a thin, hot and sour lentil soup that, when sipped and savoured, brightens the day wonderfully.

NOTE: As tamarind paste varies from brand to brand, add it gradually until it tastes good to you.

Serves **4** as part
of a main course

150g red lentils
1 teaspoon cumin seeds
3cm ginger, chopped
3 cloves of garlic, peeled
  and chopped
1 green finger chilli
2 tablespoons rapeseed oil
15 fresh curry leaves
1 teaspoon mustard seeds
¾ teaspoon ground
  black pepper
4 large ripe tomatoes, chopped
1½ teaspoons tamarind paste
1¼ teaspoons salt (or to taste)

Wash the lentils in cold water until the water runs clear, cover with water and leave to one side.

In the meantime, roughly grind the cumin seeds with a pestle and mortar, tip on to a plate, then grind the ginger, garlic and green chilli to as fine a paste as you can (or whizz in a blender).

Put the oil into a lidded saucepan over a medium heat and, when hot, add the curry leaves, mustard seeds, ground cumin seeds and black pepper. When the leaves crackle and turn translucent, carefully remove a few to decorate the rasam with later. Then add the ginger, garlic and green chilli paste to the pan. Cook for 3 minutes, then add the tomatoes. Cook for around 4 minutes, until they start to break down and become jammy.

Drain the lentils and add them to the pan with the tamarind paste and 800ml of hot water. Cover with the lid, simmer for 20 to 25 minutes, until the lentils are completely soft, then season with the salt.

The soup should be hot (but not too hot) and sour. Transfer into bowls, top with the crispy curry leaves, and either drink on its own or serve with steamed basmati rice.

GUJARATI DAL WITH
PEANUTS + STAR ANISE

This dal is my and every other Gujarati's taste of home. One spoonful and I am transported. It has a more complex taste than most dals due to the subtle jabs of star anise, curry leaves and lemon, all rounded off with the sweetness of honey. Because of the time it takes to soak and cook toor lentils, this is more of a weekend dish in our house, although a daily staple across Gujarat.

Serves **4 as part
of a main course**

300g yellow toor lentils
2 star anise
rapeseed oil
½ teaspoon mustard seeds
¾ teaspoon cumin seeds
4 whole cloves
1 green finger chilli,
  slit lengthways
2 sprigs of fresh curry leaves
3 large ripe tomatoes, chopped
½ teaspoon ground turmeric
1⅓ teaspoons salt
2½ teaspoons runny honey
1½ tablespoons lemon juice
30g red-skinned
  peanuts, crushed

Soak the toor lentils in cold water overnight, or in warm water for an hour before cooking. When soaked, wash the lentils in a few changes of cold water until the water runs clear, then place in a saucepan and cover with 4cm of cold water. Add the star anise and set to boil over a medium heat. The lentils will take around an hour to become tender (so you can crush them easily with the back of a spoon), and you may need to remove the scum that forms, using a large spoon. While the lentils cook, you can prepare the tempering.

Put 2 tablespoons of oil into a frying pan over a medium heat. When hot, add the mustard seeds, cumin seeds, cloves, green chilli and 6 curry leaves. Stir-fry for 2 to 3 minutes, until you can smell the spices, then add the tomatoes. Cook for around 5 minutes, until the tomatoes become soft and paste-like, then add the turmeric, salt, honey and lemon juice. Cook for a couple of minutes, then turn off the heat.

When the lentils are cooked, whisk them to thicken, then add the tempering. The mixture will be quite thick, and Gujarati dal is normally thin, so add at least 200ml of hot water (or as you prefer), then simmer for a further 15 minutes. Check that the salt, lemon, chilli and honey are to your liking, then take off the heat.

Put another tablespoon of oil into a separate frying pan and, when hot, add a sprig of curry leaves and the crushed nuts. Fry until the curry leaves crisp up and the peanuts brown, then take off the heat. Transfer the dal to a serving dish and scatter over the curry leaves and the peanuts. Serve with steamed basmati rice, a green leafy vegetable curry like the savoy cabbage, black kale and potato subji on page 95, and a side of yoghurt and pickles.

(GF) (DF)

RAJMA FOR THE WHOLE FAMILY

Gujaratis love to get the whole family over, and food is always central to the occasion. The only problem is that the family is usually pretty big. There's an art to cooking for a lot of people. You need a dish that doesn't require much prep, isn't technically challenging, and doesn't have to be tended to continuously. Above all else, it has to be delicious. My pick is always rajma or kidney bean curry. It's simple to put together, yet feels both rich and festive. I've given quantities for four and forty people here.

NOTES: You will need to soak the beans the day before you make this, and you'll also need a blender.

Serves **4 as a main course**

240g dried kidney beans
2 brown onions, diced
1 x 400g tin of plum tomatoes
1 green finger chilli
4cm ginger, peeled and
    roughly chopped
3 cloves of garlic
2 tablespoons rapeseed oil
½ teaspoon cumin seeds
½ teaspoon chilli powder
¾ teaspoon ground cumin
¼ teaspoon ground turmeric
¾ teaspoon ground coriander
1 teaspoon salt (or to taste)

Serves **40**

2.4kg dried kidney beans
3kg brown onions, diced
8 x 400g tins of plum
    tomatoes
8 green finger chillies
200g ginger, peeled and
    roughly chopped
25 cloves of garlic
250ml rapeseed oil
5 teaspoons cumin seeds
3 teaspoons chilli powder
6 teaspoons ground cumin
2 teaspoons ground turmeric
6 teaspoons ground coriander
6–10 teaspoons salt (to taste)

It's best to cook the 40-person dish in two batches, halving the ingredients of the recipe to cook in two large pots and tasting as you go. The quantity of salt and chilli powder are purposefully under what they should be in the 40-person recipe to allow you to adjust the final flavours yourself.

First wash the beans. If any of them float in the water, remove them. Soak overnight, and the next day place in a big pot for which you have a lid, cover with fresh cold water and bring to the boil over a medium heat. Boil for 10 minutes, then cover with a lid, reduce the heat and simmer for up to an hour until tender (though please note that the larger batch may take up to an hour longer to cook), adding water to top the pot up if necessary. Then drain, saving the boiling water for later.

In the meantime, put the onions, tomatoes (and their liquid), green chillies, ginger and garlic into a blender and whizz to a fine consistency. Pour the oil into another large pot (big enough to hold the beans) over a medium heat. When hot, add the cumin seeds and the blended paste. Cook for around 30 minutes, until the paste becomes rich, thick and a few shades darker, stirring every now and then. Then add the chilli powder, ground cumin, turmeric and ground coriander. Cook for a further 5 minutes.

Tip the beans into the pot and add 500ml of the water used to cook the beans for the 4-person serving, and 4 litres of the water for the 40-person serving. Cook for another 10 minutes, then taste and adjust the salt, chilli and consistency as you wish, and serve with a very big salad, a litre of yoghurt and lots of pickles.

LIFESAVER LENTILS

I ate this dish outside Amber Fort, one of Rajasthan's most breathtakingly beautiful palaces, but perhaps it was memorable because it was very nearly my last meal before I got caught between a fort wall and an elephant. There's a small possibility that the lively, cooling flavours in the salad quickened my senses enough for me to get away in the nick of time, in which case there's a toothless old man chopping tomatoes just outside the palace I still need to thank.

I like to eat this for lunch with bread, but it's also a lovely accompaniment to aubergine curries, or the courgette kofta on page 78. The sprouted lentils can be bought from most big supermarkets, or you can make you own (see page 289).

Serves 2 as a main course
or 4 as a side

2 tablespoons rapeseed oil
1 large red onion, thinly sliced
4 tablespoons lemon juice
2 green finger chillies, finely
  chopped
2 cloves of garlic, minced
200g ripe baby tomatoes,
  halved
1 teaspoon ground cumin
1¼ teaspoons salt
500g sprouted lentils or
  mung beans
40g fresh coriander, finely
  chopped

Put the oil into a frying pan over a medium heat and, when hot, add the red onion. Cook for 5 minutes, then add the lemon juice and fry for another 5 minutes.

Next, add the green chillies and garlic and fry for 3 minutes, until the raw smell of the garlic disappears. Then add the tomatoes and 6 tablespoons of water and fry for 5 minutes until jammy, stirring frequently. Add the ground cumin and salt, followed by the sprouts, and mix well. Fry for 3 minutes, until the sprouts have warmed through, then add the chopped coriander. Stir and take off the heat.

Delicious with buttery naan bread and yoghurt as a simple meal for two, or as part of a bigger spread.

LENTIL FRITTERS WITH YOGHURT + CHUTNEYS

(dai wada)

Makes 25 (serves 6 to 8
as a snack)

FOR THE FRITTERS
250g split urad dal, or white lentils
1½ green finger chillies,
roughly chopped
5cm ginger, peeled and
roughly chopped
1¼ teaspoons salt
½ teaspoon ground turmeric
½ teaspoon cumin seeds
rapeseed or sunflower oil

FOR THE RED
PEPPER CHUTNEY
3 cloves of garlic
2 tablespoons tomato ketchup
⅓ teaspoon salt
2 red peppers, diced
2 tablespoons lemon juice
⅓ teaspoon chilli powder
up to 2 teaspoons sugar

FOR THE DATE CHUTNEY
100g dates, stoned
½ teaspoon ground cumin
¼ teaspoon salt
2½ teaspoons tamarind paste
(or to taste)

FOR THE YOGHURT DRESSING
500ml Greek yoghurt
1 teaspoon sugar
½ teaspoon salt
seeds of 1 pomegranate (see
page 289 for how to deseed)
20g fresh coriander, leaves
picked and chopped

Every mum has a special party dish. This is my mum's. I've seen it come out at birthdays, anniversaries and weddings, and there is a good reason for this – all our family and friends badger her to cook it. After frying, the fritters are traditionally dipped in water, covered in yoghurt and then coated in chutney. But I prefer my fritters crunchy, so (with Mum's permission) I've left that step out.

NOTE: You'll need a blender for the chutneys.

Wash the dal in a few changes of cold water until the water runs clear, then leave to soak for 6 hours or overnight. When the dal has finished soaking, make the chutneys. Place all the ingredients for the red pepper chutney in a blender and whizz to a fine consistency, adding a couple of tablespoons of water if need be. Transfer to a bowl. Then blend all the ingredients for the date chutney, along with 100ml of water, and transfer to a bowl. To make the yoghurt dressing, put the yoghurt into a bowl, and add the sugar and salt along with 75ml of water. Stir to mix. Cover and refrigerate both the chutneys and the dressing.

To make the fritters, drain the dal and place in a blender or food processor. Add the green chillies, ginger, salt, turmeric and cumin seeds, and pour in up to 200ml of water, adding it little by little until the batter is a hummus-like consistency. Place a high-sided frying pan over a medium heat at the back of the hob, then pour in 4cm of oil. You'll know it's ready when you put a bit of the mix in and it floats to the top – or use a thermometer and wait for it to reach 180°C. Have a plate lined with kitchen paper standing by.

Scoop up a generous teaspoonful of batter and scrape it into the oil with another teaspoon. Move around with a slotted spoon for 2 to 4 minutes, until it turns an almond colour, then drain and place on the kitchen paper. Taste for texture and flavour: it should be fluffy inside, so if it's doughy increase the cooking time, and adjust the salt and chilli as you see fit. Fry 10 or 12 at a time until you've used all the batter. Place the fritters on a large platter. Spoon over the yoghurt, dot with the red pepper chutney and follow with the date chutney. Finally, scatter over the pomegranate seeds and top with the chopped coriander. Serve immediately.

(PULSES)

GF

RICE

Rice is the most important cereal food of half the human race, but cooking it confounds some of the most confident cooks I know, my own husband included. His fear struck deep when, just before serving it to friends one time, it congealed into a sticky porridge.

Because of its basic life-sustaining qualities, in India it is revered as a symbol of auspiciousness. It features heavily in blessings: at weddings in the hope of adequate food for newly married couples; in new homes in the hope of prosperity and happiness; and it is one of the first things to be cooked in a new Indian kitchen, in the hope of good food.

Far from being just an accompaniment to curry, with a few ingredients and Indian ingenuity, a pilau or biryani is a meal in its own right and often the centrepiece of a feast.

Although there are thousands of different varieties of rice, from Himalayan Red to Ambe Mohar (mango blossom) rice, I tend only to eat basmati, for its smell, clean flavour and slenderness in comparison to the other types of rice commonly available here. I also buy it in enormous 15kg bags, which makes it very economical to eat regularly.

If you are one of the fearful, you needn't be. Here are a few tips and tricks that should make cooking rice a stress-free and reliable event for you (unless you're my husband, in which case I am on hand).

FOUR STEPS TO FOOLPROOF RICE

MEASURE BY THE MUG

I was taught that a mugful (an average coffee mug) will feed four people as an accompaniment. But because, like all Indians, I love to over-feed people, I usually cook a mug and a half.

ALWAYS WASH AND SOAK

Rice is very starchy, and it's this that makes it gloopy. Washing and soaking helps to remove the starch – it's the first thing I do before I start cooking. To wash the rice, place it in a bowl and pour cold water over the top. Shake your hand in the bowl, watch the water cloud up, drain, and repeat until the water is clear. Then leave to soak for 20 minutes in cold water, or 10 minutes in warm water if you can't wait that long.

STEAM OR BOIL

There are two schools of thought on cooking: you can either steam it or boil it. If you're steaming it, use one and a half times the volume of water to rice, so one and a half mugs of water to every mug of rice. Put the rice and water into a pan, bring to the boil, cook for 2 minutes, then cover with a tight-fitting lid, reduce the heat and simmer for 10 minutes. If you're boiling it, cover with plenty of cold water, bring to the boil, lower the heat to a fast simmer and cook for 10 minutes. It's done when it's tender and there's no longer a chalky core.

ALWAYS LET IT REST

No matter how you cook it, rice loves to rest after all that cooking. It gives it a chance to recover and for the grains to separate. Try not to skip this step – it will make a big difference to how nice and fluffy your rice becomes.

(RICE)

A TRADITION OF EXCELLENCE
ROYAL®
BASMATI RICE
FROM THE FOOTHILLS OF THE HIMALAYAS
NATURALLY AROMATIC
PREMIUM AGED
DISTRIBUTED BY
©KUSHA INC., 2010 - IRVINE, CA 1-800-550-7423
Ⓤ NET WT. 20 LB. (9.07 kg) PRODUCT OF INDIA

GARDENERS' QUESTION TIME PILAU

I love to listen to BBC Radio 4 when I'm cooking: it's a soothing backdrop to all the frenetic chopping, frying and clattering that can happen in my kitchen. Once upon a *Gardeners' Question Time*, a member of the audience asked for suggestions for what to do with an overabundance of summer greens. I remember thinking that it was a good question, and made this dish as an answer: a bountiful pilau, substantial, flavoursome, but light enough for a summer's evening. So if you're reading this, Mr Trusty of Guildford, this is for you.

NOTE: Only add the broad beans if you have the tenacity to shell them; if not, just add more peas.

Serves 4 to 6 as a main course

300g basmati rice
200g broad beans
450ml hot vegetable stock
2 tablespoons rapeseed oil
1 teaspoon cumin seeds
4cm cinnamon stick
2 large onions, finely sliced
3cm ginger, peeled and grated
4 cloves of garlic, crushed
2 green finger chillies,
    finely sliced
400g broccoli florets,
    4cm across
200g courgettes, sliced
200g peas (fresh or defrosted)
1 teaspoon ground black pepper
1⅓ teaspoons salt (or to taste)
10g fresh dill
10g fresh mint leaves
lemon wedges, to serve

Wash the rice in a few changes of cold water until the water runs clear, then leave to soak for 20 minutes, or in warm water for 10 minutes if you can't wait that long. In the meantime, remove the beans from their pods and place in a pan. Cover briefly with boiling water, then drain and place in a pan of cold water. Squeeze each one gently to remove its thick outer skin.

When the rice has soaked, make up the vegetable stock and pour into a deep lidded saucepan. Drain the rice, then add to the stock and bring to the boil. Cook for 2 minutes, then cover with the lid, turn the heat down and simmer for 10 minutes. Turn the heat off and leave to rest and steam.

Put the oil into a large lidded pan over a medium heat and, when hot, add the cumin seeds and cinnamon stick. Leave to sizzle until fragrant, then add the onions. Cook for 6 to 8 minutes, until the onions are translucent and softening but not yet coloured, then add the ginger, garlic and green chillies and cook for another 5 minutes, stirring occasionally.

Add the broccoli florets to the pan, stir to mix, then add 5 tablespoons of water and cover immediately so the broccoli can steam through. After 2 minutes add the courgettes and a couple more tablespoons of water, and after another couple of minutes add the broad beans, peas, black pepper and salt. Cook for another minute or two, then take the mixture off the heat and fold in the rice. You might need to delicately break up the clumps of rice using your hands.

Once the greens and rice are mixed, check the salt, then transfer to a serving dish. Tear up the herbs and sprinkle over. Serve with wedges of lemon and yoghurt or a raita, like the beetroot raita on page 248.

MAHARAJAH'S RICE

Using only the most expensive ingredients one can get one's royal hands on, this is good with other feasting dishes like the roast cauliflower korma on page 68.

Serves 4 as part
of a main course

300g basmati rice
100g dried soft fruit
  (e.g. apricots and dates)
20 strands of saffron
50g chopped nuts (e.g.
  pistachios and almonds)
25g unsalted butter
4 whole cloves
10 black peppercorns
4cm cinnamon stick
½ teaspoon salt

Wash the rice in a few changes of cold water. When the water runs clear, leave to soak in a bowl of cold water for 20 minutes.

Next, boil the kettle, put the dried soft fruit into a bowl and cover with hot water. In a separate bowl, soak the saffron strands in 2 tablespoons of water.

When the rice has finished soaking, place a lidded saucepan over a medium heat. When hot, put the chopped nuts into the pan and toast them for a minute or two until they turn a shade darker, then remove to a plate. Melt the butter in the same pan, then add the cloves, black peppercorns and cinnamon. When the cloves and black peppercorns swell and smell lovely, drain the rice and add to the pan along with the salt.

Stir to coat the grains in butter, then pour in 400ml of tap water. Bring to the boil, cook for 2 minutes, then cover with the lid, turn the heat down and simmer for 10 minutes. In the meantime, drain the fruit and chop it into small pieces.

When the rice is cooked, leave to rest for 5 minutes, then fluff up with a fork. Fold in the dried fruit and nuts, and drizzle over the saffron in its soaking liquid.

(RICE)

GF

TAMARIND + CARAMELIZED RED ONION RICE

(imli chawal)

A very simple way to create a flavourful rice that's a great accompaniment to many of the dishes in this book – particularly coconut curries, like the Keralan vegetable istoo on page 89 and the pumpkin and black-eyed bean curry on page 169. It is also an absolute hit with dogs, judging by how quickly mine wolfed down an entire bowl of it when I accidentally left it out on the side. Dogs are less fussy about what's served with the rice.

NOTE: As tamarind pastes varies from brand to brand, add it gradually, adding more if need be, until the sweetness of the onions and the sourness of the tamarind are balanced.

Serves **4 as a side**

300g basmati rice
1 tablespoon sesame seeds
3 tablespoons coconut or
   rapeseed oil
10 fresh curry leaves
2 red onions, halved and
   thinly sliced
1½ teaspoons cumin seeds
½ teaspoon ground
   black pepper
2 teaspoons tamarind paste
   (or to taste)
1¼ teaspoons salt
½ teaspoon chilli powder

Wash the rice in a few changes of cold water. When the water runs clear, leave to soak in cold water for 20 minutes, or in warm water for 10 minutes if you can't wait that long.

In the meantime, place a large frying pan over a medium heat and, when hot, add the sesame seeds. Toast for a couple of minutes until golden brown, then tip into a small bowl. Put the oil into the same pan. When hot, add the curry leaves. When the curry leaves crackle, add the red onions and cumin and cook for 15 minutes, until the onions are really soft, golden and sweet. Stir through the black pepper, tamarind paste, salt and chilli powder, then take off the heat and leave to one side.

Drain the rice and transfer to a deep saucepan. Cover with plenty of cold water and bring to the boil. Lower the heat to a fast simmer and cook for 10 minutes or until the rice is tender and not chalky. Drain, then cover with a clean tea towel and leave to steam for 5 minutes, until lovely and fluffy.

Using a fork, transfer the rice into the pan with the onions. Put the pan back on the heat and fold the rice into the onions until it's fully mixed and hot. Mix in the sesame seeds, take off the heat and serve.

(GF) (DF) (VE)

LEMON RICE WITH PEANUTS + CURRY LEAVES

(nimbu chawal)

I'm a huge fan of any recipe where the end result far outweighs the effort of making it. Lemon rice is one of those dishes. The sweet, smoky shallot, lemon and peanut mixture can easily be knocked up while you wait for the rice to cook.

I like to eat it by itself or with a little tomato rasam (see page 177) for a simple meal. If you're serving it as part of a bigger spread, it's great with sambhar (page 173) or Keralan vegetable istoo (page 89), and mighty nice with a fish curry too.

Serves **4 as a side**

300g basmati rice
3 tablespoons rapeseed oil
1 teaspoon black mustard seeds
20 fresh curry leaves
3 tablespoons unsalted
   peanuts, preferably
   red-skinned
2 green finger chillies,
   slit lengthways
4 banana shallots, halved
   and finely sliced
½ teaspoon ground turmeric
2 tablespoons lemon juice
1¼ level teaspoons salt

Wash the rice in a few changes of cold water. When the water runs clear, leave to soak in cold water for 20 minutes, or in warm water for 10 minutes if you can't wait that long. Drain the rice and transfer to a deep saucepan. Cover with plenty of cold water and bring to the boil. Lower the heat to a fast simmer and cook for 10 minutes or until the rice is tender and not chalky. Drain, then cover with a clean tea towel and leave to steam for 5 minutes, until lovely and fluffy.

Put the oil into a large frying pan over a medium heat and, when hot, add the mustard seeds. When they begin to pop, add the curry leaves, peanuts and green chillies. Stir-fry for a minute or two, then add the shallots.

Cook the shallots for 10 to 12 minutes, until they are soft, caramelized and sweet. Turn the heat down low, add the turmeric, lemon juice and salt, stir to mix, then add the rice. Fold through until it's well mixed, and serve.

FRESH COCONUT RICE WITH CASHEWS + SHALLOTS

(kaju nariyal chawal)

This would be one of my desert island dishes, partly because I assume most desert islands have a plentiful coconut supply (and the odd frying pan), but also because it is good enough to eat just by itself. It's also one of the few dishes where you can't substitute desiccated coconut for fresh, because there are so few ingredients in the first place you'd notice the difference in texture.

Serves 4 as a side

300g basmati rice
rapeseed oil
75g cashews
100g fresh grated coconut (see page 92 for how to do this)
optional: 2 teaspoons chana dal
1 teaspoon mustard seeds
12 fresh curry leaves
4cm cinnamon stick
200g banana shallots, finely sliced
2cm ginger, peeled and grated
1 green finger chilli, finely chopped
1 teaspoon salt

Wash the rice in a few changes of cold water. When the water runs clear, leave to soak in cold water for 20 minutes, or in warm water for 10 minutes if you can't wait that long.

In the meantime, put a teaspoon of oil into a large frying pan over a medium heat and, when hot, add the cashews and fresh coconut. It is important to have a watchful eye here, as the coconut catches very easily. Stir-fry for a couple of minutes, until the cashews are burnished and the coconut is flecked golden brown, then tip out into a bowl and leave to one side.

Drain the rice and transfer to a deep saucepan. Cover with plenty of cold water and bring to the boil. Lower the heat to a fast simmer and cook for 10 minutes or until the rice is tender and not chalky. Drain, then cover with a clean tea towel and leave to steam for 5 minutes, until lovely and fluffy.

Put 3 tablespoons of oil into the same pan and, when hot, add the chana dal (if using), the mustard seeds, curry leaves and cinnamon stick. When the curry leaves crackle and the mustard seeds pop, add the shallots, ginger and green chilli. Cook for 10 to 12 minutes, until the shallots are caramelized and dark brown. Remove a heaped tablespoonful of cooked shallots and leave to one side to decorate the finished dish, then put the cashews and coconut back into the pan, along with the salt, and stir to mix. Using a wooden spoon, gently fold in the rice. You may need to break up any clumps with your hands beforehand.

Tip on to a serving plate and scatter the reserved shallots over the top.

DAYBREAKER KEDGEREE

(kitchari)

I can't think of a better daybreaker than fried onion rice with seared portobello mushrooms and runny poached eggs.

Serves 4 as a main course

300g basmati rice
10g dried mushrooms
　(e.g. porcini)
butter
10 fresh curry leaves
4cm cinnamon stick
½ teaspoon ground black pepper
2 brown onions, sliced
4 cloves of garlic, crushed
250g portobello mushrooms,
　sliced 1cm thick
1 teaspoon garam masala
1 teaspoon ground cumin
　(plus extra to serve)
½ teaspoon ground turmeric
1 teaspoon salt (plus
　extra to serve)
20g fresh coriander, finely
　chopped (plus extra to serve)
2 tablespoons lemon juice
4–8 medium eggs

Wash the rice in a few changes of cold water. When the water runs clear, leave to soak in cold water for 20 minutes, or in warm water for 10 minutes if you can't wait that long. Place the dried mushrooms in a small bowl and cover with 100ml of freshly boiled water.

Put 25g of butter into a wide lidded frying pan over a medium heat. When it starts to bubble, add the curry leaves, cinnamon stick and black pepper. Stir for a minute, then add the onions and garlic. Turn the heat down and cook for 20 minutes, stirring occasionally.

Meanwhile, put a tablespoon of butter into a separate frying pan over a medium to high heat. When hot, add as many portobello mushroom slices as will fit without them touching. Fry for 2 minutes, then turn the mushrooms over, fry again for a minute or two, then slide on to a plate. Repeat until all have been cooked.

Drain the dried mushrooms, but keep the soaking water. Roughly chop and discard any tough stems. Gently pour the mushroom stock into a measuring jug, leaving the last tablespoon behind, as it can be very gritty. Top up with tap water to make 450ml of liquid.

When the onions have turned a lovely caramel colour, add the garam masala, cumin, turmeric and salt. Stir to mix, then add the drained rice, chopped dried mushrooms and mushroom stock. Cover the pan with the lid, bring to the boil, then turn the heat down and simmer for 20 minutes. Stir through the coriander, lemon juice and portobello mushrooms. Taste and readjust the seasoning if need be, then put the lid back on to allow the rice to rest for 5 minutes.

Now poach the eggs. Fill a wide saucepan with water and bring to the boil. Stir the water, break the eggs into the pan, turn the heat down to a simmer and cook for 2 minutes for a soft yolk or up to 4 minutes for a firm yolk. While the eggs are poaching, divide the rice between plates or bowls. Remove the poached eggs with a slotted spoon and lay over the top. Sprinkle with salt, cumin and a little extra chopped coriander, then serve.

GF

RHEA'S POTATO + ONION POHA

(kanda batata poha)

Rhea is Mum's friend Praful's nephew's wife. She is Maharashtrian and lives in Mumbai. She often makes this for the family for breakfast, but it's easily lovely enough for lunch or dinner. Poha is partially cooked and flattened rice. It's a magical ingredient which doesn't need soaking like basmati does, and cooks quickly. You can buy it from Asian grocery stores or online.

Serves 2–4 for breakfast

240g thick poha
3 tablespoons unsalted
  peanuts, preferably
  red-skinned
2 tablespoons rapeseed oil
1 teaspoon cumin seeds
½ teaspoon mustard seeds
1½ green finger chillies,
  finely sliced
12 fresh curry leaves
2 medium red onions, halved
  and finely sliced
200g Desiree potatoes, peeled
  and cut into 1cm cubes
½ teaspoon ground turmeric
1¼ teaspoons salt
2 tablespoons lemon juice
2 tablespoons desiccated or
  fresh grated coconut

Put the poha into a sieve and run cold water over it for a full minute. Move the grains around delicately with your hand to ensure they're all wet through.

Place a large lidded frying pan over a medium heat and, when hot, add the peanuts. Stir-fry for 1 to 2 minutes, until browning, then transfer to a plate.

Put the oil into the same pan over a medium heat and, when hot, add the cumin and mustard seeds, green chillies and curry leaves. When the curry leaves crackle, add the red onions. Cook for around 6 minutes, until the onions are translucent, then add the potato cubes.

Stir-fry the potatoes for a minute, then add 4 tablespoons of water, cover with the lid and cook for 4 minutes. Uncover, add a little more water if need be to stop the potatoes from sticking, and cook for another 4 minutes, or until completely tender.

Add the poha to the pan, along with the turmeric, salt, lemon juice, coconut and another couple of tablespoons of water. Stir to mix, then turn the heat to low, cover with the lid and cook for around 10 minutes, until the rice is cooked.

Check the salt and lemon juice and adjust as you wish. Serve with hot ginger chai (see page 280).

  (VE)

LIME PICKLE RICE WITH ROASTED SQUASH

(nimbu achar kaddoo ka chawal)

If this is the first recipe you turned to in this book because you love lime pickle so dearly, welcome. You have found a kindred spirit in me. For the uninitiated, lime pickle is hot, salty and with so much punch that you'll be left trying desperately to open your eyes for a minute after your first bite. That being said, when it is stirred through rice and accompanied by sweet roast squash and red onions, its wings are clipped, in a good way. Serve to other pickle lovers, with more lime pickle on the side.

Serves 4 as a main course

1 large butternut squash
   (around 1kg)
rapeseed oil
250g basmati rice
salt and ground black pepper
20g ghee or unsalted butter
3 cloves of garlic, thinly sliced
½ teaspoon cumin seeds
½ teaspoon nigella seeds
½ teaspoon fennel seeds
½ teaspoon mustard seeds
1 large red onion, sliced
2 tablespoons good lime
   pickle, like Patak's
4 spring onions, thinly sliced

Preheat the oven to 220°C/425°F/gas 7 and line a couple of roasting trays with foil.

Cut the squash in half lengthways, deseed, then slice into 2cm-thick semicircles. Drizzle with just enough oil to coat the pieces and sprinkle with salt and black pepper. Place on the trays and roast for around 40 minutes, until cooked through and starting to colour.

Wash the rice in a few changes of cold water. When the water runs clear, leave to soak in cold water for 20 minutes, or in warm water for 10 minutes. Drain the rice and transfer to a deep saucepan. Cover with plenty of cold water and bring to the boil. Lower the heat to a fast simmer and cook for 10 minutes or until the rice is tender and not chalky. Drain, then cover with a clean tea towel and leave to steam until needed.

Put a large frying pan over a medium heat and, when hot, add the ghee, followed by the sliced garlic and the spices. Stir-fry until the garlic turns golden and sticky, then add the red onion. Cook for around 10 minutes, until the onion is soft and starting to brown, then add the pickle and season with salt to taste. Stir and add the roast squash. When the squash is warmed through, add the rice and stir to mix. When hot, take off the heat and sprinkle the spring onions over the top.

Serve with a bowl of yoghurt and a salad.

(RICE)

GF

GRAND VEGETABLE BIRYANI

(mast biryani)

This is a love letter to humble vegetables. It's a meal for special occasions, whether that be Diwali, Christmas or a bar mitzvah. It's packed full of a rainbow of colours, flavours and textures, from spiced paneer, chickpeas and tomatoes to roasted beetroots, sweet potatoes and a citrusy coconut and coriander sauce. It's not a difficult recipe, far from it, but it's definitely one to take your time over.

NOTE: You will need a blender, and also a medium casserole dish or biryani dish – around 24cm in diameter is perfect.

Serves 6 as a main course

400g basmati rice
400g sweet potatoes
400g raw beetroot
500g ripe tomatoes
1 x 400g tin of chickpeas,
    drained
225g hard paneer, cut
    into 2cm cubes
rapeseed oil
salt
1¼ teaspoons chilli powder
1¼ teaspoons ground cumin
2 teaspoons garam masala
2 tablespoons lemon juice
2 large onions, finely sliced
1 egg
300g ready-rolled puff pastry
1 tablespoon sesame seeds
1 tablespoon nigella seeds

Preheat the oven to 200°C/400°F/gas 6 and line three baking trays with foil. Wash the rice in a few changes of cold water, then leave to soak.

Next, wash the sweet potatoes and beetroot well (no need to peel them) and cut into wedges around 6cm x 2cm. Put them on separate trays. Cut the tomatoes into quarters, then eighths. Place them on the final baking tray and add the chickpeas and cubes of paneer.

Put 6 tablespoons of oil into a small bowl with 1⅓ teaspoons of salt, the chilli powder, cumin, garam masala and lemon juice. Mix well, then spoon over the vegetables, adding more to the tomato and paneer tray than the other two. Make sure everything is evenly coated, then put the trays in the oven – with the paneer on the top shelf – and bake for 40 minutes, checking and stirring after 20 minutes.

In the meantime, put 3 tablespoons of oil into your casserole or biryani dish over a medium heat. When hot, add the onions and fry for 15 to 20 minutes, until really soft, brown and caramelized, stirring regularly. Remove to a bowl and keep the dish to one side.

1 x 400ml tin of coconut milk
100g fresh coriander,
    roughly chopped
6 cloves of garlic
1 green finger chilli
3cm ginger, peeled
¾ teaspoon salt
2 tablespoons lemon juice

While the onions are cooking, place all the ingredients for the coconut and coriander sauce into a blender and whizz to a fine consistency. Pour it into a frying pan (make sure to scrape down the sides of the blender) over a medium heat and cook for 10 minutes, stirring every now and then. Check the salt and take off the heat.

Next, drain the the rice and place in a deep saucepan. Cover with plenty of cold water and bring to the boil. Lower the heat to a fast simmer and cook for 10 minutes or until the rice is just tender. Drain well, cover with a clean tea towel and leave to one side. Break the egg into a small cup, add a generous pinch of salt and whisk with a fork.

Now you are ready to layer your biryani. The aim is to end with a rice layer topped with caramelized onions. First, put half of the paneer, tomato and chickpea mixture into the bottom of the pot. Follow with a quarter of the rice and a quarter of the onion mix. Then add half of the coconut and coriander sauce and half of the beetroot and sweet potatoes, then a further quarter of the rice and onions. Repeat, finishing with a final layer of rice and onions.

Cut a square of puff pastry to fit over the top of your pot. Working quickly (as you need to keep the pastry as cold as possible), press it down tightly around the edges of the pot. Brush the top liberally with the beaten egg, and sprinkle with the seeds. Place in the oven for 25 minutes.

Gingerly take out of the oven and place on the table. Cut the pastry away and discard to reveal the steamy biryani. Serve big spoonfuls so that everyone gets good colourful layers, alongside a bright beetroot raita (see page 248) or cucumber and mint raita (page 247), and a salad like the leaves, herbs and curds (page 140).

TOMATO + GREEN BEAN SEVAI

(thakkali sevai)

Sevai are rice noodles that are incredibly popular in South India, particularly in Karnataka and Tamil Nadu. They're eaten for breakfast, as a snack in the day, and even for dinner. I like to cook these when I'm looking for something light, quick and zingy to eat.

Serves 2 as a main course

coconut oil
250g green beans, topped
  and tailed
10 fresh curry leaves
½ teaspoon black
  mustard seeds
1 red onion, thinly sliced
3 cloves of garlic,
  very thinly sliced
1½ green finger chillies,
  very finely chopped
250g ripe tomatoes, each cut
  into 8 wedges
⅓ teaspoon salt
½ teaspoon ground
  black pepper
300g fresh thin rice noodles
juice of ½ a lemon

Place a large lidded frying pan over a medium to high heat. When hot, put a teaspoon of coconut oil and half the beans into the pan. Leave to cook for 2 minutes without stirring to give them a chance to blister and char, then toss and cook for another 4 minutes, until tender, tossing halfway through. Tip the beans on to a plate and cook the other half in the same way, removing to the plate when ready.

Next, put 2 tablespoons of coconut oil into the same pan over a medium heat and, when hot, add the curry leaves and mustard seeds. When they pop and crackle, add the red onion. Cook for 10 minutes, until the onion is soft and golden, then add the garlic and green chillies and cook for another 4 minutes. Add the tomato wedges and cover with the lid. Cook for a further 5 minutes, until the tomatoes become jammy and soft, then add the salt and black pepper.

Put the noodles and the green beans into the pan and toss through. Squeeze over the lemon juice and adjust the seasoning if need be, then serve.

AUTUMN PILAU WITH AUBERGINES, TOMATOES + CHICKPEAS

Some things never go out of fashion – this combination of aubergines, tomatoes and chickpeas is one of them. This is an excellent dish for a cold autumn day which always hits the spot.

Serves 4 as a main dish

250g basmati rice
rapeseed oil
3 medium aubergines (roughly
    900g), halved and cut into
    1cm slices
50g unsalted butter
1 large onion, thinly sliced
5 cloves of garlic, crushed
400g ripe plum
    tomatoes, chopped
⅓ teaspoon ground cinnamon
¾ teaspoon ground
    black pepper
1½ teaspoons ground cumin
¼ teaspoon ground cloves
1⅓ teaspoons chilli powder
1½ teaspoons salt (or to taste)
1 x 400g tin of chickpeas,
    drained
375ml vegetable stock

Wash the rice in a few changes of cold water until the water runs clear, then leave to soak.

Meanwhile, put 4 tablespoons of oil into a large frying pan over a medium to high heat. When hot, add a small batch of the aubergines, just enough to lay on the bottom of the pan without crowding. Cook for 6 to 8 minutes, until soft, collapsing and (hopefully) nicely browned on the outside, turning every couple of minutes. Transfer to a plate, then fry the rest, adding more oil per batch.

In the same pan, melt the butter, add the onion and fry for around 8 minutes. Remove a tablespoonful of onion to scatter over the top of the rice later. Add the garlic to the pan, fry for a couple of minutes, then add the tomatoes. Cook for around 5 minutes, until the tomatoes are softened, then add the cinnamon, black pepper, cumin, cloves, chilli powder and salt. Stir well, then add the chickpeas and the aubergines. Cook for a couple of minutes, and take it off the heat.

Pour the vegetable stock into a deep saucepan with a tight-fitting lid. Drain the rice, add to the vegetable stock and bring to the boil. Cook for 2 minutes, then cover with the lid, turn the heat right down and simmer for 10 minutes, or until tender. Turn the heat off and let the rice steam through for 5 minutes. Fluff up the rice using a fork before folding in the aubergines and chickpeas. Mix well and heat together for a couple of minutes, then take off the heat.

Transfer to a serving dish, scatter over the reserved onion and serve with a cooling dollop of yoghurt and a little pickle on the side.

MENU IDEAS

With any sort of cuisine. the big question is what to eat and how to pull it all together. Here are some suggestions.

EVERYDAY DINNER FOR TWO
Keralan vegetable istoo
Tamarind and caramelized red onion rice
Cucumber and mint raita
Salted jaggery kulfi with bananas

FOUR FRIENDS FOR DINNER
Chestnut mushroom and walnut samosas
Beetroot pachadi
Goan butternut squash cafreal
Rice
Pan-fried pineapple with cardamom ice cream

DRINKS PARTY NIBBLES
Sticky mango paneer skewers
Chestnut mushroom and walnut samosas
The Queen's Bombay nuts
Home-made poppadoms with tomato masala
Cashew nut fudge

A FEAST
Beetroot shami kebabs
Grand vegetable biryani
Cauliflower korma with blackened raisins
Sri Lankan dal with coconut and lime kale
Leaves, herbs and curds
Cucumber and mint raita

GUJARATI MENU
Dhokla
Baby aubergines stuffed with peanut and coconut
Moong dal with a garlic and cumin tarka
Chapattis
Chewy date and nut balls

SOUTH INDIAN MENU
Keralan vegetable istoo
Beetroot pachadi
Tamarind and caramelized red onion rice
Smashed pineapple and turmeric raita

NORTH INDIAN MENU
New potato and chickpea chaat
Rajma for the whole family
Paneer butter masala
Rice, chapattis, pickles
Carrot halwa with garam masala pecans

BREADS

At the heart of every Indian kitchen is the daily bread.

In most Gujarati homes (and mine) that daily bread is the chapatti: a deliciously soft, charred, wholemeal flatbread. Making them is incredibly meditative and so addictive: the feel of the flour, the binding of the dough, the smell that fills the house as they bake on the stove. Wherever I am when I make them, I feel at home. (I have included my chapatti recipe from *Made in India* in the 'How To' section on page 288.)

If I'm not making chapattis, I'm usually making another Gujarati classic, thepla (see page 215). I'll never forget the time my Aunty Palvani left a flight attendant red-faced when she slapped down some thepla and achar (pickle) over the top of my in-flight meal. 'Much better for you than plane food,' she said, before offering the flight attendant some too. Otherwise known as 'journey bread' (because it travels well), thepla is made from chickpea flour and sesame seeds, and is tasty enough to be eaten all on its own.

Punjab is the breadbasket of India. Its rich soil and a healthy supply of river water result in an abundance of corn and wheat. One of the most popular breads is makki ki roti: cornmeal bread (see page 217), often served with freshly churned butter and mustard greens. Punjabis are champion tandoor cooks and are well known for their whopping great elephant ear naans (page 220), slathered in garlic butter. To mimic their tandoori naan, I turn the heat to the highest temperature in my oven, which works a treat.

To the south, in Kerala, you'll find the undisputed king of parathas, the elegant Malabar (page 218). This beautiful coiled, flaky and buttery bread is nothing but pure joy to tear apart layer by layer and dip into a thick (usually coconutty) sauce.

But I cannot write about South India and bread without mentioning the dosa. The sour tang of the fermented lentil and rice is inexplicably addictive, as are the fudgy coconut potatoes that often fill them. To share my love of dosa, I've created a quick, weekday version (page 222), and a more rigorous recipe for the real deal that is probably best left to a weekend (page 227).

Whichever bread you go for, don't worry if things are a little wonky. After all, as my mum always says, 'Taro hath besejase' – roughly translated, practice makes perfect.

SQUASHED TOMATO UTTAPAM

This dish is dedicated to making your snack times brilliant: uttapam is a cross between a pancake and a crumpet, to which you can add any vegetables. I am partial to squashed tomatoes, sweet caramelized onions and the odd chilli, and I am also not averse to Cheddar grated over the top (when no other Indians are looking).

Makes 8 (enough
for 4 to snack on)

FOR THE UTTAPAMS
150g rice flour
100g plain flour
1 teaspoon bicarbonate of soda
⅓ teaspoon salt
2 tablespoons Greek yoghurt
240ml warm water
2 medium eggs

FOR THE TOPPING
rapeseed oil
2 red onions, sliced
2 green finger chillies, slit
  lengthways
½ teaspoon salt
½ teaspoon ground black
  pepper
250g ripe baby tomatoes,
  sliced thinly

Put both flours, the bicarbonate of soda, salt and yoghurt into a bowl. Mix thoroughly, then make a well and add the water and eggs. Whisk to a smooth batter and leave to one side.

To make the topping, put 3 tablespoons of oil into a frying pan and, when hot, add the red onions. Cook for 12 to 15 minutes, until the onions have caramelized, then add the green chillies, salt and black pepper, and stir. Add the sliced tomatoes, stir again, then take off the heat.

To cook the uttapam, put 1 teaspoon of oil into a non-stick frying pan over a medium heat. When hot, pour a small ladleful of batter (around 60ml) into the pan, smooth it out into a round with the back of your ladle, and allow to set for 1 minute. Then take a tablespoonful of the tomato mixture and place it on top. Flip the uttapam and cook for another minute, or until cooked through, then shuffle on to a plate.

It's always a good idea to test a little of the first one to check the cooking times and flavour, adjusting either if need be, before cooking the rest of the uttapams.

These are delicious with a vegetable sambhar (see page 173) and coconut chutney (page 239).

CAULIFLOWER CHEESE +
CHILLI STUFFED ROTI

I love a stuffed paratha as much as the next Indian, but when life feels too short to make them, I prefer to make these, much quicker stuffed rotis. I tend to stuff them with whatever can be foraged from the fridge, which is how I found this strange and wonderful mixture. Not quite cauliflower cheese or Indian chilli cheese toasts, but somewhere in between, and sublime.

Makes 12 (enough
for 6 people)

FOR THE CAULIFLOWER
CHEESE STUFFING
500g cauliflower, broken into
rough pieces
2 tablespoons rapeseed oil
1 onion, diced
2 green finger chillies,
very finely sliced
1 teaspoon ground cumin
1 teaspoon salt
½ teaspoon ground
black pepper
150g Cheddar, grated

FOR THE ROTIS
600g plain flour
(plus extra to dust)
1 teaspoon salt
4 tablespoons oil
(plus extra for the dough)
300ml warm water

To make the stuffing, grate the cauliflower or pulse in a food processor until it's in rice-grain-sized pieces. Put the oil into a frying pan over a medium heat and, when hot, add the onion. Fry for around 8 minutes, until soft and golden, then add the green chillies and cumin. Stir-fry for a minute, then add the cauliflower and cook for 4 to 5 minutes. Stir in the salt and black pepper, take off the heat, add the cheese and stir through.

To make the roti dough, put the flour into a large bowl and mix in the salt, then add the oil and mix well. Make a well in the middle and, little by little, add the water (I use half boiled water, half cold tap water), kneading as you do so, until the dough is soft and springy. Pat with oil and leave to one side.

Flour a clean surface and divide the dough into 12 pieces. Roll each bit between your palms to form a ball, flatten it out and coat in flour. Roll into a 10cm round, then recoat both sides in flour and continue rolling out to around 20cm.

Take 2 tablespoons of the stuffing and spread it on one half of the roti, leaving a little room around the edges to seal closed by pressing down. Gently roll over the top with your rolling pin to flatten the stuffed bread, then leave to one side. Repeat.

To cook the stuffed rotis, place a frying pan on a medium to high heat. When hot, throw on the first roti and cook for around 3 minutes, turning halfway through. Press down on any uncooked bits of the roti with your spatula until cooked, then transfer to a plate. Repeat.

To keep your rotis warm while you cook the rest, make a foil nest for them to sit in and keep them in the oven on a low heat. Serve with a little pickle, such as the Mysore lemon pickle on page 245.

JOURNEY BREAD

(t h e p l a)

Gujaratis are naturally suspicious of food cooked outside of the home, and will usually carry a stash of these when they travel, alongside a small but lethal tub of garlic and chilli chutney. Unlike the daily chapatti, which was designed to be a backdrop to more flavourful things, thepla is naturally very tasty because it's made from chickpea flour and sesame seeds. It's best eaten with a little mango chutney, yoghurt and a simple dry curry or subji, like the okra and potatoes on page 81.

NOTE: Ajwain seeds are also known as 'bishop's weed' or 'carom seeds'. They are small but mighty and taste somewhere between star anise, oregano and thyme. If you can't find them, it's not a problem to leave them out.

Makes **8** (enough for 4 people)

150g wholemeal flour
   (plus extra to dust)
50g chickpea (gram) flour
1½ teaspoons sesame seeds
¼ teaspoon ajwain seeds
¼ teaspoon ground turmeric
⅓ teaspoon chilli powder
½ teaspoon salt
rapeseed oil
120ml warm water

Put both flours into a bowl along with the sesame seeds, ajwain, turmeric, chilli powder and salt. Mix thoroughly, then add a tablespoon of oil and rub through with your fingers until the flour resembles fine breadcrumbs. Make a well in the centre and, little by little, add the water (I use half boiled water, half cold tap water). Mix together, then knead for around 5 minutes to form a soft and pliable dough.

Get your rolling station ready. You will need a floured board or clean surface, ideally at the side of the stove, a rolling pin, and a bowl of flour in which to dip the balls of dough.

Next, set a good-sized pan over a medium to high heat. Divide your dough into 8 balls. Take one, coat generously with flour, and roll out to a circle around 16cm in diameter, coating it with a little flour as you need it to stop it from sticking. Put it face side down on the hot pan.

Wait for the edges to turn white and for the bread to start to bubble (which will take 30 to 45 seconds), then turn over and cook for the same amount of time. Drizzle ¼ teaspoon of oil over the bread and spread with the back of a spoon. Turn over again, dab it down with the flat side of the spatula, then sprinkle another ¼ teaspoon of oil over the bread and turn over again. Check that all the dough is cooked (any uncooked spots will look dark and doughy) and put on to a plate. Repeat.

Eat on the back seat of the car with as many family members as will fit. Or at home, with yoghurt and pickle.

CORN ROTI

(makki ki roti)

This is a gift from Punjab to you and me and everyone we know. Use it wisely, preferably as the Punjabis do, with a steaming bowl of mustard leaf saag and a spoonful of freshly churned butter. I've broken with tradition by cutting these rotis with a large cookie cutter instead of rolling them by hand, because the cornmeal can crack easily (and besides, it's much quicker).

Makes around 10 small rotis

200g fine cornmeal
100g plain flour
⅓ teaspoon salt
rapeseed oil
2 green finger chillies,
   very finely sliced
1cm ginger, peeled and grated
140ml hand-hot water

Put the cornmeal, flour and salt into a bowl and mix. Add 1 tablespoon of oil and rub through with your fingers until the flour resembles fine breadcrumbs. Then add the green chillies and ginger and stir to mix. Little by little, mix in the water – you might not need it all – and knead for around 5 minutes, until it becomes a soft and pliable dough.

Roll out half the dough on a floured surface to 5mm thick. Take a 10cm cookie cutter or a bowl with a thin rim, turn upside down and press into the dough to create discs. Do the same with the other half of the dough.

To cook the rotis, put a frying pan over a high heat, drizzle a little oil into the pan and cook 2 to 3 rotis at a time for around 3 minutes, turning every minute or so until cooked through and no darker doughy spots can be seen.

Slather with fresh home-made butter (see page 285) and eat with mustard greens (page 99).

MALABAR PARATHA

The Malabar paratha is South India's poster bread. Beautifully coiled, and flecked with charred golden spots, it manages to be flaky, crispy, soft and fluffy all at once: perfect for peeling away layer by layer and dunking into a rich, creamy sauce. Make sure to leave some time to make this bread: it needs 1 hour at the kitchen counter, 1 hour 20 minutes of resting time, and a final 30 minutes to cook the bread.

Makes 10 (enough
for 5 people)

130g unsalted butter
450g plain white flour
1¼ teaspoons salt
185ml warm water
rapeseed oil, to grease

Melt 80g of butter in a saucepan over a medium heat. Put the flour and salt into a large bowl, mix together, then add the melted butter and mix with your hands until the flour resembles breadcrumbs. Little by little, add the warm water (I use half boiled water, half cold tap water) and mix until you have a rather sticky dough.

Tip the dough on to a clean, lightly floured surface and knead for around 5 minutes until soft. Then leave in an oiled bowl covered by cling film in a warm spot for an hour.

After an hour, separate the dough into 10 balls, place on a baking tray and cover with a clean tea towel or more cling film, then leave to rest for another 20 minutes.

Prepare a rolling station by lightly oiling a chapatti board or chopping board and your rolling pin. Melt the rest of the butter in a saucepan over a medium heat. Then take a piece of dough, roll it into a ball and flatten it between your palms. Roll out to a circle around 18cm in diameter, brush the surface with butter, then roll it up into a cigar. Shape the cigar into a tight coil (which looks like a snail shell) and pop back on the tray. Repeat with the rest of the dough.

Next, take one of the coiled pieces, flatten between your palms and roll out to 18cm. Place it on a piece of greaseproof paper and roll out the rest, separating each layer with more greaseproof paper.

Place a non-stick frying pan over a medium heat. When hot, take a paratha and brush both sides with melted butter. Cook for around 2½ minutes, flipping halfway through. Paint with butter one last time, then shuffle on to a plate and repeat with the rest. To keep them warm, put them into a nest of foil and keep them enclosed until serving.

ELEPHANT EAR GARLIC NAAN

Despite being old enough to know better, I still shriek with delight in Indian restaurants when the waiter lowers the family-sized naan bread on to the table like a spacecraft landing. I particularly enjoy suddenly jostling into place as everyone tries to get the most garlicky and buttery bit. This is my Aunty Harsha's famous and incredibly reliable naan bread recipe, but transformed into a sharing oven naan bread.

Makes **4 big sharing naans**
  (for 6 to 8 people)

rapeseed oil
110g unsalted butter
4 cloves of garlic, crushed
salt
500g strong white bread flour
  (plus extra to dust)
4 tablespoons yoghurt
1 x 7g packet of dried yeast
1 level teaspoon baking powder
2 teaspoons sugar
275ml whole milk, hand hot
nigella seeds, to sprinkle

Preheat the oven to 240°C/475°F/gas 9, move a wire rack to the top of the oven, and lightly oil a large thin baking tray.

To make the garlic butter, put the butter into a small saucepan over a low to medium heat and, when melted, add the garlic and a couple of big pinches of salt. Cook for 5 minutes, then take off the heat.

Place the flour in a large bowl. Make a well and add 2 tablespoons of oil, the yoghurt, yeast, baking powder, sugar and 2 teaspoons of salt. Mix through with your fingers until the ingredients resemble breadcrumbs, then add the warm milk, little by little, and mix again until it comes together into a dough.

Place the dough on a clean and well-floured surface. The dough will be very sticky at first, soft but fairly robust. Knead for around 5 minutes, then scrape any dough off your hands, using a spoon, and settle the dough by rubbing a teaspoon of oil all over it.

Transfer the dough to a bowl in which it can double in size. Cover it with a clean tea towel or cling film, and leave in a warm place for at least an hour. (Mum leaves hers in the airing cupboard; I leave mine in an oven that's been heated to 110°C/225°F/gas ¼ for 10 minutes, then switched off.)

When the dough has risen, separate it into 4 pieces. Put 3 pieces into a bowl and cover while you roll the first. Roll it into a ball and flatten it between your palms. Roll it out with a rolling pin into a triangular shape, around 25cm long and 25cm at its widest point. Add a little oil while you're rolling if need be.

In the meantime, put the baking tray into the oven for 5 minutes. When hot, lay the naan on the tray and sprinkle with nigella seeds. Cook for 5 minutes on the top shelf, then remove. The naan should be soft, fluffy and cooked through, with no doughy spots. Brush or drizzle on the garlic butter, and repeat with the other naans. Keep them warm by creating a foil nest for them, and try not to eat them before serving.

DAILY DOSA WITH COCONUT POTATOES

(masala dosa)

In Mysore there is a little shoebox of a restaurant called Mylari Dosa that serves just two things: dosa and chutney. It doesn't sound like much, but this one is *the master*. After having gone back there a dozen times, I've tried as best as possible to replicate what I ate there, although I've devised this version so it can be cooked during the week. (For the bona fide weekend dosa recipe, turn to page 227.)

Makes **6** (serves 4 to 6 as a main course)

FOR THE COCONUT POTATOES
750g baby new potatoes
2 tablespoons rapeseed oil
1 teaspoon black mustard seeds
¾ teaspoon cumin seeds, roughly ground
optional: 2 teaspoons chana dal
12 fresh curry leaves
1 large onion, quartered and sliced
2.5cm ginger, peeled and grated
2 green finger chillies, thinly sliced
100g creamed coconut
1¼ teaspoons salt
1 tablespoon unsalted butter or ghee

FOR THE DOSAS
175g chickpea (gram) flour
75g plain flour
½ teaspoon salt
½ teaspoon bicarbonate of soda
rapeseed oil

Wash the potatoes, place in a saucepan, cover with cold water and bring to the boil. Boil for 15 to 20 minutes, until they're tender and you can slide a knife through them easily. Drain, then mash them up a bit.

Put the oil into a large frying pan and, when hot, add the mustard seeds. When the seeds pop, add the cumin seeds, chana dal (if using) and curry leaves. Stir-fry for a minute, then add the onion, ginger and green chillies. Cook for 10 to 15 minutes, until the onions are soft and golden, then add the potatoes. Stir to mix, then grate in the coconut cream and add the salt. Mix in the butter or ghee, check for seasoning, then leave to one side.

Make the dosas by putting the flours into a large bowl with the salt and bicarbonate of soda. Mix thoroughly, then slowly whisk in 380ml of water so that you have a smooth batter.

Place a 20cm frying pan over a medium to high heat. When hot, put a teaspoon of oil into the pan, swirl it around, then follow with a ladleful of batter and immediately swirl the batter around to coat the bottom. Cook for a minute, then spread a sixth of the potato mixture in a line down the middle of the dosa. Cook for a further 20 seconds to 1 minute, until the base of the dosa is crispy and the potato mixture is hot. Then slip the dosa out of the pan and roll up. Repeat with the rest of the batter. To keep the dosas warm, put them into a basket fashioned from foil, or just serve them as they come.

Eat by itself, or serve with rasam (see page 177), sambhar (page 173) or Keralan vegetable istoo (page 89), and coconut chutney (page 239).

DF VE

WEEKEND DOSA

These crispy fermented rice and lentil pancakes are more than just pancakes, they are one of India's most celebrated national treasures. They've got a lot going for them: crunchy, nicely tangy and very versatile. The only downside is that they take about 48 hours to prep properly. The best way I've found to do this so they're ready for Sunday lunch is to soak them on a Friday night, churn on Saturday morning, leave to ferment until Sunday morning and cook up at midday. Delicious with coconut chutney (see page 239) and coconut potatoes (page 222).

NOTE: You will need a blender for this recipe.

Makes 6 (enough for
  4–6 people)

275g basmati rice
60g split urad dal, or white
  lentils
½ a teaspoon fenugreek seeds
280ml warm water
1 teaspoon salt
rapeseed oil

Wash the rice and dal together in a few changes of cold water until the water runs clear, then drain. Transfer to a large heatproof bowl and add the fenugreek seeds. Pour in the warm (body temperature) water and leave to soak overnight.

The next morning, or 12 hours later, drain the rice and dal and blend in two batches. Then cover with cling film and place in a relatively cosy spot (I use the kitchen counter, or a bookshelf in my living room) for 24 hours. The next morning, whisk the batter and add the salt.

To make the dosas, put a large non-stick frying pan over a low heat until hot. Prepare a plate for the dosas, a small pot of oil with a piece of kitchen paper, and a ladle. You can test the heat of the pan by flicking a little water on to it. If it fizzes and bubbles away, it's ready.

Take the kitchen paper, dab it in the oil and wipe the surface of the pan, then pour in a sixth of the batter. Work quickly to spread the batter outwards in concentric circles, using the back of the ladle, then turn the heat up to medium. Cook for 2 minutes, until the batter leaves the sides of the pan. Dizzle a little oil around the outside of the dosa to loosen it if need be, then flip it and cook for 1½ minutes on the other side. If the dosa is nice and crispy, shuffle it on to the plate.

Remove the pan from the heat for a minute, turn the heat down low and repeat the same again. To keep the dosas warm, put them into a basket fashioned from foil, or just serve them as they come.

BANANA AND CARDAMOM BUNS

These buns are a healthier take on the addictive deep-fried Mangalorean banana puris that locals queue up for at breakfast time. They're not as sweet as you'd imagine, but perfectly sweet enough.

Makes **8**

250g plain flour
¾ teaspoon dried yeast
salt
35g caster sugar
½ teaspoon ground cardamom
   (or finely ground seeds
   from 6 pods)
3 very ripe bananas
   (150g peeled weight)
100ml whole milk
25g unsalted butter
1 egg

Preheat the oven to 190°C/375°F/gas 5.

Put the flour, yeast, ½ teaspoon of salt, the sugar and cardamom into a large bowl and stir to combine. Peel the bananas and weigh them – you will need 150g of banana for this recipe. Mash them, then add to the bowl and stir in.

Warm the milk and butter gently to body temperature (if it's too hot it will kill the yeast), then pour into the bowl. Mix until the dough comes together, then knead for 5 minutes. It will be super sticky, which is no bad thing. Cover with cling film and leave to one side until doubled in size. If you're making these for breakfast, you could do this the night before, and let the dough prove in a bowl in the fridge.

When the dough has risen, divide it into 8 pieces (each weighing around 85g). Roll each one into a neat ball, then place on a baking tray lined with baking paper, making sure you leave at least 5cm between each bun. Cover with a clean tea towel, and leave to prove until nearly doubled in size again. This might take up to 2 hours, depending on how warm your kitchen is.

When the buns are nice and plump, crack the egg into a cup, add a decent pinch of salt and mix well with a fork. Brush the egg wash over the buns, and bake in the oven for 20 minutes, or until golden brown and hollow-sounding when tapped on the bottom.

PICKLES, CHUTNEYS
+ RAITAS

A simple meal can be transformed into a culinary event with a little pickle, and so it is that these small but powerful meal-brighteners will always be found on the table or in the fridge of Indian families. My great-grandmother was famed for having a hand for pickle-making, and even now, as my grandmother tells me she forgets how to make them, her hands remember each of the steps perfectly. She has passed most of her recipes on to her daughter-in-law, Harsha, my aunt with whom she lives and from whose fridge, every evening, comes the pickle tray. It's so large that it takes up the whole top shelf, and you can almost feel a little gust of air being pushed out from underneath as it's lowered on to the kitchen table.

The pickles and chutneys on her tray and all across India are incredibly varied and run the gamut of flavours, textures and types. There are fresh chutneys, like South Indian coconut chutney (see page 239), made by grinding coconut together with chillies, salt and ginger, which are best eaten on the day you make them. Then there are gently cooked, fresh, sweet chutneys, made with seasonal ingredients like sweet mango or guava, to enjoy while the season lasts. The same ingredients, because of their short seasons, are also pickled, preserved in simple brines and oil alongside spices, to be used across the year, when a craving hits.

Despite the variety, the techniques and equipment are simple. Salt, lemon juice, spices and oil are used to preserve and pickle, and in India sunshine is often used to dry out the vegetables. You won't find any canning equipment or even thermometers in a typical Indian kitchen. There are also no long sterilization times in the oven, and there are no real best-before dates. Pickles are simply allowed to develop their own personalities, and a mother's judgement is carefully exercised on what has passed its best.

Things have changed a little in my and my mother's kitchen. We use thermometers and always sterilize jars by putting them in the dishwasher on a full cycle. We never use metal tops if the jar contains lemon juice or tamarind (as they will rust the top and spoil the pickle), and because we don't have India's fierce sunshine here, we tend to steam the vegetables instead.

In contrast to pickles and chutneys, the sole purpose of raitas is to cool and provide contrast against the heat of a curry or pickle. They are always made using yoghurt, which quickly brings welcome relief from chillies, and in my eyes, if made well, raitas can be good enough to eat by themselves with just a little bread.

ADITYA'S AUBERGINE + TAMARIND CHUTNEY

(brinjal mensakai)

I've been searching for the perfect aubergine chutney for years, and I think I've finally found it. Aditya is a good friend of mine who I worked with at Gymkhana, one of London's best Indian restaurants. Following a few months of persuasion, he finally gave me his family recipe, which comes all the way from a remote hillside village in Karnataka.

NOTES: A jam thermometer is useful for checking the oil temperature. As tamarind paste varies from brand to brand, add it gradually until it tastes good to you.

Makes a large jar (around 1kg)

750g baby round aubergines
rapeseed or sunflower oil
3 teaspoons nigella seeds
25 fresh curry leaves
10 green finger chillies,
   sliced into thirds at an angle
200ml tamarind paste
1¼ teaspoons salt

Take the tops off the aubergines, then quarter them. Place a frying pan on one of the back burners of the hob, pour in 4cm of oil and heat over a medium flame. Get a plate ready with some kitchen paper on it.

When the oil reaches 180°C, lower in a small batch of the aubergines and fry for 2 to 4 minutes, until they develop a light golden colour, then remove and place on the plate. Repeat in small batches until you've fried all the aubergines.

Put 6 tablespoons of oil into a frying pan over a medium heat and, when hot, add the nigella seeds and curry leaves. When the leaves crackle, add the green chillies. Stir-fry for a minute, then add the tamarind paste along with 200ml of water. Cook the paste until the water evaporates and the paste is quite thick, then add the salt and the fried aubergines. Stir-fry for a couple of minutes, and take off the heat.

When the chutney has cooled, transfer to a scrupulously clean jar and refrigerate. It will keep for 2 to 3 weeks in the fridge.

MRS SURA'S LEMON + RED CHILLI PICKLE

(khatta nimbu mirch achar)

A tongue-tickler of a pickle: it's fresh, bright, zesty and hot. The ajwain seeds add a distinct flavour, not dissimilar to thyme. I am partial to using this pickle to liven up sandwiches and simple subjis with its salty and sour heat. It takes a couple of days to make and then will keep for 2 months in the fridge.

Makes a medium jar (around 400g)

4 lemons (300g net lemon flesh)
100g cayenne or slim red chillies
1 teaspoon ground turmeric
1 teaspoon ajwain or carom seeds
3½ teaspoons salt

First you'll need to peel your lemons. Take a small paring knife, cut off both ends of each lemon and sit it upright. Gently wedge the knife between the skin and the flesh of the lemon and cut down into the pith, following the lemon's natural curve. Continue all the way around, then gently cut or peel away the pith until you're left with the lemon flesh.

Cut the flesh into quarters, then slice each quarter into 0.5cm pieces (you can take out the seeds if you wish). Then chop the chillies very finely.

Place the chillies and lemons in a non-reactive bowl (like glass or ceramic) and add the turmeric, ajwain and salt. Mix thoroughly with a clean spoon, then cover with a clean cloth.

Keep the pickle out on the side, but out of direct sunlight, and stir twice a day for the next 2 days. The mixture will soften and collapse a bit. Transfer to a sterilized jar and press down with the back of a spoon.

HARSHA AUNTY'S
GREEN CHILLI + MUSTARD PICKLE

(rai wara mircha)

Adding pungent mustard to hot chillies doesn't sound as though it should work, but the combination is sublime. A couple of days' fermenting with some lemon juice and salt really rounds the edges off the chillies and creates a champion worthy of a daily spot on the kitchen table. I like to eat this with soft-boiled eggs first thing in the morning.

Makes a small jar (80–100g)

4 teaspoons yellow
  mustard seeds
80g green finger chillies
2 level teaspoons salt
½ teaspoon ground turmeric
4 tablespoons rapeseed oil
2 tablespoons lemon juice

Crush the mustard seeds with a pestle and mortar until most of the seeds have split in half, then place in a non-reactive bowl (like glass or ceramic). Halve the green chillies and cut into 5cm pieces, then place in the bowl and add the rest of the ingredients. Mix well and keep out on the counter, covered with a clean tea towel, for two days, stirring once or twice a day, then transfer to a sterilized jar.

This pickle will keep in the fridge for up to a month. It's delicious with everything, but especially dal, chapattis, eggs, vegetable subjis and also in ham sandwiches.

FRESH COCONUT CHUTNEY

Fresh, creamy, hot, and the perfect accompaniment to the dosas on pages 222 and 227. This is a fresh chutney, so it won't keep long and ideally needs to be made on the day of eating.

NOTE: You will need a blender for this recipe.

Serves 2

1 green finger chilli
125g fresh coconut
  (see page 288)
2cm ginger, peeled
⅓ teaspoon salt
1 tablespoon rapeseed oil
10 fresh curry leaves
1 teaspoon mustard seeds

Whizz all the ingredients together in a blender with 150ml of hot water, and taste. It should be creamy and sweet, with a balanced level of salt and a soft heat, so adjust as you wish before serving.

GUNPOWDER

This is a very clever chutney. It's essentially a powder which you bring to life by adding it to equal parts oil, then mixing it all up. It's got a deeply savoury toasted chickpea flavour and is hot without being ear-tinglingly so. It's usually eaten with dosas or mixed in with rice. I like to sprinkle the powder over green beans, or drizzle the chutney over hot pillowy naan bread.

NOTE: You will need a blender for this recipe.

Makes a small jar
  (around 150g)

150g roasted chana dal
  (daria dal)
2 teaspoons rapeseed oil
1 teaspoon cumin seeds
½ teaspoon asafoetida
3 teaspoons chilli powder
2 teaspoons salt

Put a frying pan over a medium heat. When hot, tip in the dal and swirl it around for 3 minutes, then remove to a bowl. Put the oil into the frying pan over a medium heat and, when hot, add the cumin seeds. Stir-fry for a minute or two until brown, then add the asafoetida, chilli powder and salt. Stir to mix, then take off the heat.

Put the roasted chickpea dal and the cumin mix into a blender and whizz to a powder. You might need to push the mixture down the sides more than a couple of times until it's all powdered. Leave to cool, then transfer to an airtight container. It will last for around 6 months when stored in a cupboard.

PUNJABI PICKLED RADISH, CARROT + CAULIFLOWER

(punjabi achar)

Hot, salty and vinegary, this addictive pickle can perk up the dullest of things.

Makes a large jar
  (around 750g)

½ a small cauliflower (250g)
200g radishes
2 medium carrots
120ml rapeseed oil
1 tablespoon mustard seeds
3 whole Kashmiri chillies,
  broken into pieces
1 teaspoon ground turmeric
3½ teaspoons chilli powder
350ml Sarson's distilled
  spiced pickling vinegar
3 teaspoons salt
3 teaspoons sugar

Break the cauliflower into small florets no more than 2cm in diameter and transfer to a bowl. Top and tail the radishes and carrots, then peel the carrots and slice both very thinly with a mandolin or a knife, and add to the bowl.

Put the oil into a casserole dish that's big enough to fit all the vegetables, and place over a medium heat. When hot, add the mustard seeds, and when the seeds pop, add the Kashmiri chillies. Stir-fry for a minute, then add the turmeric and chilli powder. Stir, turn the heat down and add the vinegar.

Cook for 10 to 15 minutes over a medium to low heat until it reduces down to a balsamic-like consistency, then add the salt, sugar and sliced vegetables. Stir to mix, then immediately take off the heat.

Transfer to an exceptionally clean or sterilized jar, making sure all the vegetables are covered with the pickling liquid. Keeps for a month in the fridge.

PINEAPPLE + GINGER CHUTNEY

(ananas ki chatni)

In Kolkata there is a restaurant called Kasturi that has no menu. The chef there cooks some of the best food I've had, and always serves this pineapple and ginger chutney to boot. It really does go with anything – I've eaten it with fish, meat and dosas, and it makes a wonderful sandwich filling with Cheddar, ham or fish.

Makes a medium jar
  (around 350g)

1 medium ripe pineapple
2 tablespoons rapeseed oil
3 teaspoons black
  mustard seeds
3cm ginger, peeled and grated
¾ teaspoon chilli powder
1 teaspoon ground black pepper
1¼ level teaspoons salt
125g sugar
juice of 2 limes

Cut off the top and the base of your pineapple and discard, then stand the pineapple upright and cut away the skin from top to bottom. If there are 'eyes' still left in the sides, gouge them out with the tip of a knife. Now cut the flesh of the pineapple away from the round fibrous core in the middle, then dice up the flesh.

Put the oil into a large non-stick frying pan over a medium heat. When hot, add the mustard seeds, and when the seeds start to pop, add the ginger, chilli powder, black pepper, salt and diced pineapple. Mix well and cook for around 20 minutes, stirring occasionally.

Add the sugar and lime juice and cook for a further 15 to 20 minutes, until the pineapple looks translucent and soft and all the liquid has reduced and looks a bit like jam.

Taste and adjust the salt, sugar or lime as you wish, then transfer into a scrupulously clean jar. This chutney will keep for at least a couple of weeks in the fridge.

RHUBARB + GINGER CHUTNEY

In this time of being able to access most fruit and veg all year round, forced rhubarb remains staunch in only making a brief appearance each year from late January to April. When it does, I want to preserve as much of it as possible, but despite my best intentions, this chutney never lasts very long.

Makes a medium jar
(around 400g)

1 dried Kashmiri chilli
1½ tablespoons rapeseed oil
½ a star anise
3 whole cloves
3cm cinnamon stick
½ teaspoon black peppercorns, roughly ground
¼ teaspoon ground cardamom (or finely ground seeds from 3 pods)
50g ginger, peeled and very finely chopped
400g rhubarb, cut into 3cm pieces
1½ tablespoons lemon juice
60g caster sugar
½ teaspoon salt

Chop the Kashmiri chilli into tiny pieces and keep to one side.

Put the oil into a large frying pan over a medium heat and, when hot, add the star anise, cloves, cinnamon stick and chilli pieces. When the cloves puff up in the hot oil, add the black peppercorns and cardamom. Stir to mix, then add the ginger. Cook for 3 minutes, then add the rhubarb, lemon juice, sugar and salt. Leave to cook for 6 minutes, or until just tender but not mushy.

Take off the heat and check the sugar, salt and lemon juice – it should be sweet, hot and sharp, so add more if need be. Leave to cool and transfer to a clean jar. This chutney will keep for up to a week in the fridge.

MYSORE LEMON PICKLE

(nimbu achar)

This is a wonderful pickle. Tangy, pungent and delicious, it's long-lasting too.

Makes a large jar (around 1kg)

1kg lemons
120ml rapeseed oil
30 fresh curry leaves
2 teaspoons mustard seeds
½ teaspoon fenugreek seeds
2cm ginger, peeled and grated
5 cloves of garlic, sliced
4 green finger chillies,
  sliced into thirds at an angle
1½ teaspoons ground turmeric
30g salt
2 teaspoons chilli powder

Quarter each lemon, then quarter again. Sit the lemon pieces in one layer on a steamer over a medium heat, and steam for 8 to 10 minutes, until tender. Remove and keep to one side.

Put the oil into a frying pan over a medium heat. When hot, add the curry leaves, mustard seeds and fenugreek seeds. When they crackle, add the ginger, garlic, green chillies, turmeric, salt and chilli powder and stir-fry for a couple of minutes.

Finally, add the steamed lemons. Stir-fry for another couple of minutes, then take off the heat. Leave to cool, and transfer to a very clean or sterilized jar, where it will keep for a month.

SOUR MANGO + JAGGERY CHUTNEY

(gor keri)

This chutney is a Gujarati favourite, made when the first mangoes of the season arrive. I asked my 83-year-old grandmother to show me how to make it. 'I don't remember how to,' she said, but amazingly, her hands rhythmically chopped the mango and stirred in the spices – she did it automatically and didn't have to stop to think once. It made her nostalgic. She said her mum and she used to pickle together, and said I must pickle with my daughters and that I must hurry up and have daughters, then broke into a sly wink.

Makes **a large jar**
(around 600g)

1kg unripe green mangoes
(around 600g net weight)
1 teaspoon salt
½ teaspoon ground turmeric
4 tablespoons rapeseed oil
1 teaspoon mustard seeds
¾ teaspoon chilli powder
210g jaggery (or to taste)

Wash the mangoes but don't worry about peeling them. Cut off the fatter 'cheeks', slicing as close to the central stone as possible, followed by the chunks of flesh on the other sides of the stone. Then salvage whatever other flesh you can.

Chop it all into 1cm cubes and transfer to a bowl, along with ½ teaspoon of salt and the turmeric. Mix together and set aside for 10 minutes.

Then put the oil into a lidded frying pan over a medium heat and, when hot, add the mustard seeds. When the seeds pop or wriggle in the oil, add the mango and cover with a lid. Cook for around 8 minutes, until the skins turn a darker colour and the mango is tender, then add the remaining salt and the chilli powder. Stir, then add the jaggery a little at a time – you might not need all of it.

Cook for around 5 minutes, until the jaggery has melted and thickened, then take off the heat. Check the chutney for salt and chilli, then transfer to a clean jar and leave to cool before refrigerating. This chutney will keep for a week or two in the fridge.

FRESH PICKLED TURMERIC

(kaachi haldi achar)

This is a great delicacy, and also a pickle with a purpose. Turmeric has been heralded as a hero in the kitchen, a fighter against all ills. A little of this earthy pickle on your plate will go a long way. Watch out when you're cooking with it, though: turmeric will stain everything bright yellow, so wear gloves and an apron or face the consequences.

Makes a small jar (200g)

100g fresh turmeric root
2 tablespoons lemon juice
½ teaspoon salt

Scrape off the turmeric skin with a teaspoon or a vegetable peeler, then cut the root into 0.25cm slices. Place in a sterilized jar along with the lemon juice, salt and 100ml water. Although this is a fresh pickle, it will last for a month or two in the fridge.

CUCUMBER + MINT RAITA

(kheera ka raita)

Serves 4 as a side
  (and can be doubled easily)

1 teaspoon cumin seeds
  (plus extra to serve)
200g cucumber (plus extra
  to serve)
250ml Greek yoghurt
10g fresh mint leaves, shredded
⅓ teaspoon salt

Place a frying pan over a medium heat and, when hot, add the cumin seeds. Toast the seeds for 3 to 4 minutes, until chocolate coloured, shaking the pan every now and then to ensure they toast evenly. Then lightly grind with a pestle and mortar.

Grate the cucumber and place in a sieve. Squeeze out as much water as you can over the sink, and put the cucumber in a bowl.

Add the yoghurt, mint leaves, salt and ½ teaspoon of the cumin. Mix together, then grate a little cucumber over the top and sprinkle with a little more cumin before serving.

GF

SMASHED PINEAPPLE + TURMERIC RAITA

(ananas haldi ka raita)

A new pretender to the raita throne is this sweet, hot, earthy number. Sunshine in a bowl.

Serves 4 as a side

1 tablespoon rapeseed oil
1 teaspoon black mustard seeds
200g fresh pineapple, cut into
   small chunks
2–3 teaspoons caster sugar
1 tablespoon lemon juice
⅓ teaspoon ground turmeric
½ a green finger chilli
250ml full fat Greek yoghurt
⅓ teaspoon salt

Put the oil into a frying pan over a medium heat. When hot, add the mustard seeds, and when the seeds pop, add the pineapple. Stir-fry for around 4 minutes, until the pineapple starts to soften and turn translucent. Then add the sugar, lemon juice, turmeric and green chilli, and cook for another minute. Take off the heat and transfer to a bowl.

Smash the pineapple with a fork so that it disintegrates and becomes juicy. Add the yoghurt and salt, then taste and adjust the sugar and salt if need be.

BEETROOT RAITA

(chukandar ka raita)

This beetroot raita is loud and proud in colour and flavour. I like to eat it just by itself with a little naan, or as an accompaniment to kebabs, dals or greens.

Serves 4 as a side
   (and can be doubled easily)

2 tablespoons rapeseed oil
1 clove of garlic, sliced wafer thin
200g raw beetroot, peeled
   and grated
250ml Greek yoghurt
1 tablespoon lemon juice
⅓ teaspoon salt
½ teaspoon black mustard seeds
optional: 8 fresh curry leaves

Put a tablespoon of oil into a frying pan over a medium heat and, when hot, add the garlic. Stir-fry for a minute, until it turns pale gold, then add the beetroot. Stir-fry for 3 minutes, until it softens, then add to a bowl with the yoghurt, lemon juice and salt. Mix together.

Next make a tarka, or dressing. Put the other tablespoon of oil into the pan and, when very hot, add the mustard seeds, and the curry leaves if using. When the mustard seeds pop and the curry leaves turn translucent and crispy, take off the heat and pour over the raita.

Serve as it is, and stir when at the table.

GF

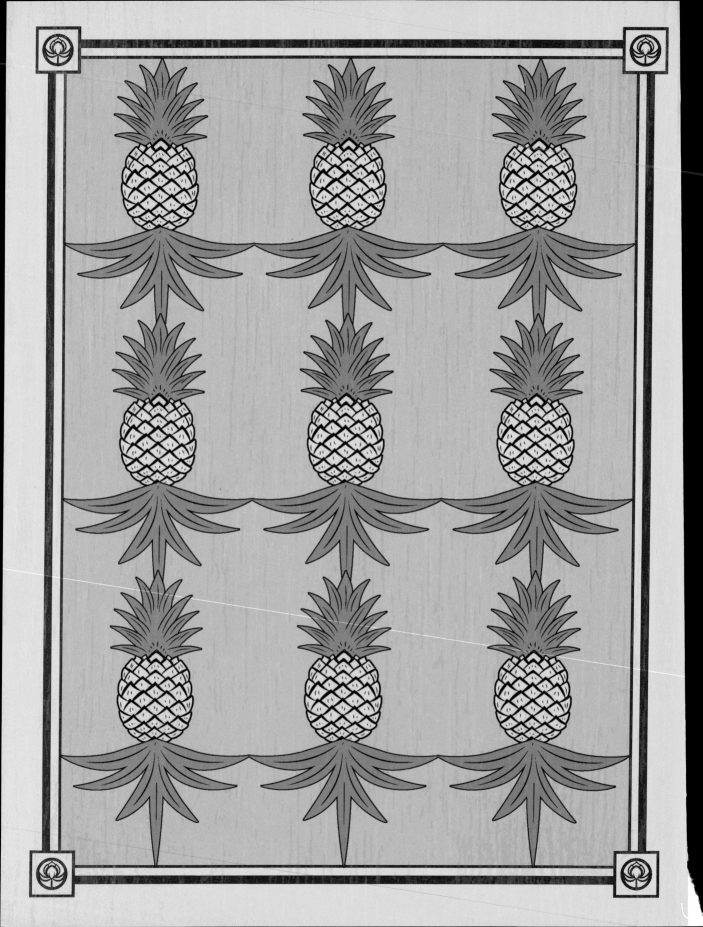

PUDDINGS

When I was a kid, we'd often stop by Bobby's Restaurant in Leicester on the way to visit my grandma and grandpa. I'd hold my breath, hoping Mr Lakhani, the owner, would be there, because like an Indian BFG he would slowly bend down in front of me and open his enormous hands to reveal a precious piece of silver foil-topped treasure: kaju katli, a smooth and creamy cashew fudge – so rich and sweet, it had to be nibbled slowly, by the crumb. I knew then that this was the start of a battle with temptation over Indian sweets.

Back then it was the sweeter the better, and Indian sweets were as sweet as their names: googras, cham chams, ladoos and jalebi. They weren't (and still aren't) reserved just for after dinner, but eaten throughout the day and between mealtimes, at the temple after being offered to the gods, and particularly on auspicious occasions and birthdays. When I got married this year, as part of the wedding ceremony, I fed my new husband sweets as a symbolic gesture to sweeten our married life ahead.

Indian sweets have mostly evolved out of ordinary kitchen ingredients. There are the famous fudgy round 'besan ki ladoos', made with chickpea flour; puddings made with rice ('kheer'), nuts, coconuts and dates, spun into something more delicious than the sum of their parts; and a hundred other sweets made with lavish quantities of milk, curd and ghee in reverence to the holy cow.

Now that I'm in my thirties, although I still have a wayward sweet tooth, my palate is changing and I prefer to balance the sweetness with something else, whether it's citrus or other fruit, spice, nuts or sometimes even salt. And while I've recorded a lot of traditional labour-intensive techniques that my grandma uses to this day – like boiling milk down to two-thirds of its original volume for a couple of hours, stirring continuously in order to make either carrot pudding or kulfi – I have found other, quicker paths to get the same flavour by using cream or condensed milk.

So in this section you will find a lot of traditional recipes to make peace with my inner child – like cashew nut fudge (see page 271), carrot halwa (page 268), gulab jamuns (page 260) and kulfi (page 257) – but all amended slightly to just the way my family and I like them.

RHUBARB + GINGER

You can serve this rhubarb in a few different ways. I prefer to eat it with yoghurt, sometimes with some 'nankatai' (see page 267), or shortbread, crumbled over the top. Or, if I want something a bit more special, I whip up some double cream and add a drop or two of rose water and sugar to make a quick rose water cream.

Serves 4

100g caster sugar
1½ teaspoons ground ginger
½ teaspoon ground cardamom
   (or finely ground seeds
   from 6–8 pods)
800g rhubarb, cut
   into 4cm pieces
yoghurt, to serve

Preheat the oven to 180°C/350°F/gas 4.

Put the sugar, ginger and cardamom into a bowl and mix together. Place the rhubarb in an ovenproof dish, and sprinkle over the sugar and spice mix, making sure the rhubarb is evenly coated. Cover with foil and bake until tender – this could take anything from 15 to 30 minutes, depending on the thickness of the rhubarb. Keep checking every 10 or so minutes, as you want the rhubarb to keep its shape.

When the rhubarb is tender, take out of the oven and leave to cool, then remove from the dish with a slotted spatula. If the syrup is watery, pour into a small saucepan and reduce over a medium heat until thicker.

To serve, gently spoon the rhubarb into serving bowls, add a dollop of yoghurt and drizzle the rhubarb syrup over the top.

PAN-FRIED PINEAPPLE WITH CARDAMOM ICE CREAM

The joy of this pudding is in the beautiful contrast of the spiced, hot, tropical pineapple with the cold, sweet, exotic cardamom ice cream. I tend to whip this up after dinner when friends come over, because the ice cream can be made in advance and the fried pineapple in 5 minutes (and the end result looks far more impressive than the effort required).

NOTES: You'll need to begin this pudding a day ahead to allow time for the ice cream to freeze. An ice-cream maker will make life easier too.

Serves 8

300ml whole milk
300ml double cream
1¾ teaspoons ground cardamom
   (or finely ground seeds
   from 20 pods)
150g caster sugar
5 egg yolks
1 large ripe pineapple
1 tablespoon unsalted butter
2 tablespoons honey
1 tablespoon lime juice
a pinch of ground cloves
seeds of 1 pomegranate (see page
   289 for how to deseed)

If you're making the ice cream by hand, clear a big space in your freezer for a large, flat plastic container. If you're using an ice-cream machine and you need to freeze the bowl beforehand, put it in the freezer now. Pour the milk, cream and cardamom into a saucepan and heat gently until small bubbles start to appear around the rim of the milk, but it's not yet boiling, stirring frequently. Take the pan off the heat and leave to infuse for 15 to 20 minutes.

Strain the mixture to sieve out the cardamom seeds. Then whisk the sugar and egg yolks together in a mixing bowl until pale and fluffy. Very slowly whisk the cream mixture into the eggs and sugar. Pour all the mixture back into a saucepan on a very low heat, stirring constantly until the mixture coats the back of a spoon, then take off the heat. Whatever you do, don't let the custard boil, as you'll end up with sweet, cardamom-y scrambled eggs.

Leave to cool in the fridge overnight, then either churn in an ice-cream machine or pour into a plastic container and freeze, beating furiously once every 30 minutes for 3 hours, or until frozen solid.

To make the pan-fried pineapple, cut off the top and the base of your pineapple and discard, then stand it upright and cut away the skin from top to bottom. If there are 'eyes' still left in the sides, gouge them out with the tip of a knife. Cut the pineapple into quarters lengthways. Remove the hard core from each quarter, then cut each into four, to make 16 wedges.

Put the butter into a large frying pan over a medium heat and, when hot, add the pineapple wedges. Turn every couple of minutes until they start to caramelize and brown, then add the honey, lime juice and cloves. Stir-fry for another minute and take off the heat. Serve the pineapple alongside a scoop of cardamom ice cream and scatter liberally with pomegranate seeds.

GF

SALTED JAGGERY KULFI
WITH BANANAS

(gur ki kulfi kela ki saath)

Jaggery is one of my special weapons in the kitchen. It's a gorgeous, deeply toffee-flavoured, fudge-like sugar made from the unrefined sap of date palms or sugar cane. It also lends itself well to a little salt, which brings out an inexplicable deliciousness.

NOTE: You will need kulfi moulds or small freezable bowls.

Serves 6

FOR THE KULFI
130g jaggery
300ml evaporated milk
300ml double cream
¼ teaspoon salt

FOR THE BANANAS
40g salted peanuts
3 bananas
1½ tablespoons rapeseed
    or coconut oil
2 tablespoons honey

Heat the jaggery in a saucepan, stirring until it melts. Then whisk in the evaporated milk and cream. When the milk and cream are fully incorporated, add the salt and bring the heat up to almost boiling, then take off the heat. Allow to cool, then pour into moulds and freeze.

When you're ready to eat, coarsely crush the salted peanuts with a pestle and mortar. Peel the bananas and cut into 1cm slices at an angle. Put the oil into a frying pan over a medium heat and, when hot, add the bananas. Drizzle the honey over the top, and try not to stir so the bananas have a chance to caramelize. Fry for 1 minute or so on each side until golden brown, then place on a plate.

If you'd like to remove the kulfis from their moulds, dip them into hot water for a second, then turn them upside down over a plate and give them a sharp tap with a spoon. Place the bananas alongside or over the top. Scatter over the salted peanuts, and serve immediately.

BENGAL BAKED CURD
WITH TAMARIND BERRIES

(mishti doi jamun ki sath)

My dad's favourite pudding is cheesecake. While the rest of us plan our meals around mains, he's already sidled up to the dessert trolley. American style, Italian and even Greens Original (the packet stuff): he loves them all. But this year, I thought I'd create a special sort of Indian cheesecake for him, using yoghurt instead of cheese. This is a variation on a Bengali set yoghurt called 'mishti doi'; the finished dish tastes similar to cheesecake but is much lighter – still rich and creamy, just not as dense. The tamarind berries and nuts add a sharp and crunchy contrast.

Happy 65th birthday, Dad.

NOTES: You'll need to make this a few hours ahead of serving so that the yoghurt has time to set. You'll also need four small ramekins.

Serves **4**

250ml Greek yoghurt
200ml condensed milk
150ml double cream
50g ground almonds
10g unsalted butter
sugar
300g mixed berries
    (e.g. raspberries,
    blueberries and
    strawberries)
1 teaspoon tamarind
    paste (or to taste)

Preheat the oven to 150°C/300°F/gas 2.

Pour the yoghurt, condensed milk and double cream into a bowl and whisk until fully mixed, then divide between the ramekins.

Place the ramekins in a deep roasting tray and pour enough just-boiled water around them to reach two-thirds up their sides. Bake for 25 minutes, then remove from the oven, leave to cool, and refrigerate for a couple of hours until set.

When set, put the almonds, butter and 1½ teaspoons of sugar into a non-stick saucepan over a medium heat. Stir continuously for a couple of minutes until the almonds start to brown and form big crumbs, then tip into a bowl.

To make the tamarind berries, cut any larger berries (like strawberries) to the same size as the smaller ones. Tip them into a saucepan along with 2 tablespoons of sugar, 3 tablespoons of water and the tamarind paste. Heat for 2 to 3 minutes, until the berries start to soften. Taste, as you may need to add more sugar depending on your berries, then take off the heat.

You can either serve the berries warm or cold, but I prefer to serve them cold. To assemble the baked yoghurts, spoon over the tamarind berries and sprinkle with the toasted almonds.

GULAB JAMUNS IN SAFFRON SYRUP

Diwali is great for two reasons. It's a celebration of good over evil, and it's the one time of the year that dentists and doctors in the Indian community keep quiet while the rest of us wade thigh-deep into our sugar-spun fantasies, eating googras, cham chams, kaju katli and kulfi. My pick of the bunch will always be these gulab jamuns. Pretty little milky doughnuts, they're a burnished bronze on the outside, white and cakey inside, and soaked to the core with delicately flavoured rose syrup. Hold me back. The pleasure of these is not only in the eating: you can make them well in advance and the gulabs will sit happily in the fridge for up to a week before your friends and family arrive.

NOTES: You will need a jam thermometer for this recipe. You'll also need full fat milk powder, which can be bought easily in an Asian supermarket or online.

Makes around 40 gulab jamuns
  (enough for 20 people)

500g caster sugar
½ tablespoon cardamom seeds
  (from 20 pods)
2 teaspoons rose water
  (or to taste)
275g full fat milk powder
  (I like Fudco or Natco)
70g self-raising flour
1 tablespoon coarse semolina
1 teaspoon ghee or butter
200ml warm milk
1 litre sunflower oil, for frying
100g pistachios, chopped
  or ground

First make a simple sugar syrup. Put the sugar, 750ml of water, the cardamom seeds and rose water into a deep-sided pan, and bring to a boil over a medium heat. Turn the heat down and simmer for around 10 minutes, until it thickens into a light, cordial-style syrup, stirring every now and again. Take off the heat, leave to cool, then taste and add more rose water (sparingly) if needed.

To make the jamuns, mix together the milk powder, flour, semolina and ghee in a bowl. Little by little, add the warm milk to the mixture to bind it together into a dough – you might not need all the milk, so add it slowly until you get a soft, pliable dough. Don't overwork it, just knead it until it comes together.

Pour the oil into a deep-sided pan and heat it to around 140°C. Meanwhile, place a large plate or tray covered with kitchen paper on the side. Roll the dough into little balls the size of a marble (around 10g each) and lay them out on another tray. These will inflate in the hot oil, so don't panic if you think they're a little small. When rolling, you might need a dab of warm ghee or oil to get a good ball. Try not to press too hard, and do your best to smooth out any cracks so the balls don't split in the hot oil. But equally, be gentle on yourself if this is your first time.

Fry 4 to 6 jamuns at a time for 5 to 7 minutes, until golden brown, or the colour of almond skin. Remove to the tray covered with kitchen paper and drain. It's worth testing the first batch. They'll be firm on the outside and cakey inside but not gooey. (If they're gooey, increase the cooking time.) Fry the rest. After they have cooled a little, put them into the syrup and leave to soak for a day or at least a few hours. To serve them warm, place the gulab jamuns and their syrup in a saucepan over a gentle heat. Serve drained of all but a couple of tablespoons of the syrup. Sprinkle ove the pistachios. If not serving straight away, refrigerate.

PISTACHIO + ALMOND CAKE WITH SAFFRON ICING

This is a rich cake for a celebration.

Serves 6

100g ground pistachios
100g ground almonds
100g self-raising flour
½ teaspoon bicarbonate of soda
150g caster sugar
½ teaspoon ground cardamom
    (or finely ground seeds
    from 6 pods)
½ teaspoon ground cinnamon
zest of 1 lemon
2 tablespoons milk
120g unsalted butter, melted
    (plus extra to grease)
3 medium eggs

FOR THE SAFFRON
CREAM FROSTING
a big pinch of saffron
100g icing sugar
75g unsalted butter, softened
100g cream cheese
30g pistachios,
    roughly chopped
a small handful of dried edible
    flowers (e.g. marigolds
    or rose petals)

Preheat the oven to 180°C/350°F/gas 4 and line a 20cm to 22cm cake tin with lightly greased baking paper.

Put the pistachios, almonds, flour, bicarbonate of soda, caster sugar, cardamom and cinnamon into a bowl and mix thoroughly. Add the lemon zest, milk and melted butter. Mix again, then beat the eggs in one by one until they're incorporated. Transfer to the cake tin and bake for 25 to 35 minutes, until a skewer comes out clean, then leave to cool.

To make the saffron cream, place a tablespoon of just-boiled water into a small bowl with the saffron and leave to infuse for 5 to 10 minutes (the longer the better). Put the icing sugar and butter into a bowl, and beat until smooth, light and fluffy. Add the cream cheese, along with the saffron in its soaking liquid. Mix until just incorporated and keep in the fridge until needed.

When the cake has completely cooled, spread the saffron cream over the top and scatter over the pistachios and edible flowers.

EAST AFRICAN PEANUT CAKE

Mum talks fondly about a cake that was made by an Ismaili Gujarati friend of hers back in Uganda. Neither her friends nor she had ovens, so they used to take the mixture down to a baker in the East Nile District and go for a swim or play with baby crocodiles while it baked. No one has a record of the recipe, but I've created this cake in its memory.

NOTE: You will need a spice grinder or food processor to grind the peanuts.

Serves **8**

180g butter, melted
  (plus extra to grease)
150g roasted unsalted peanuts
200g self-raising flour
½ teaspoon baking powder
200g caster sugar
3 medium eggs

FOR THE TOPPING
80g crunchy peanut butter
100g icing sugar
100g unsalted butter
50g salted peanuts,
  roughly crushed

Preheat the oven to 180°C/350°F/gas 4. Grease a 22cm to 24cm cake tin with butter and line with baking paper.

Grind the unsalted peanuts as finely as possible in a spice grinder or food processor. Put the flour and baking powder into a large mixing bowl, then add the caster sugar, melted butter, eggs and finely ground peanuts. Whisk to a smooth consistency.

Transfer to the cake tin and bake for 25 to 30 minutes, until a skewer comes out clean, then place on a wire rack to cool.

Meanwhile, make the icing. Beat together the peanut butter, icing sugar and unsalted butter until it's nice and smooth. When the cake has cooled completely, spread the icing over the top. I prefer the home-made 'rustic' vibe with cakes, but you can smooth the icing over with a palette knife if you prefer. Top with the crushed salted peanuts.

VERMICELLI MILK PUDDING WITH SAFFRON MANGOES

(mithi sev aam ki saath)

This recipe is based on my mum's go-to dinner party classic, which she's been serving in the same crystal bowl for decades. It's never once let her down. It's made by poaching roasted wheat vermicelli in milk and cardamom, which creates something as comforting but not quite as rich as a rice pudding. I've updated her recipe by adding some ripe mango coated in saffron and honey, sharpened with a little lemon juice.

Lusciously ripe mangoes are best in this dish, and you can buy lots of types of wheat vermicelli. It doesn't really matter which one you buy, but I tend to use the fine, long, hooked strands rather than the broken pieces for this pudding.

Serves 4

2 large mangoes
70g thin wheat vermicelli
  noodles
25g ghee or unsalted butter
750ml whole milk
½ teaspoon ground cardamom
  (or finely ground seeds from
  6 pods)
⅓ of a nutmeg, grated
50g caster sugar
a big pinch of saffron strands
2 tablespoons honey
1 tablespoon lemon juice
20g pistachios, roughly
  chopped

Peel the mangoes, then cut off the fatter 'cheeks', slicing as close to the central stone as possible, followed by the chunks of flesh on the other sides of the stone. Then salvage whatever other flesh you can. Chop it all into 1.5cm cubes.

Next, break up the noodles into small strands around a thumb-length long. Melt the butter in a saucepan over a low heat, then add the noodles to the pan. Stir-fry for 3 or 4 minutes, until the noodles turn almond brown – they can burn easily, so keep a watchful eye over them – then take off the heat.

Let them cool for a minute or two, then add the milk and put the pan over a low to medium heat. Simmer for 10 minutes, stirring every now and again. The mixture will thicken and bubble – when it does, turn the heat right down and add the cardamom, nutmeg and sugar. Stir well and remove from the heat.

To make the saffron mangoes, put a couple of tablespoons of water into a small saucepan over a low to medium heat and add the saffron strands. When the saffron starts to colour the water, add the honey. Wait for the mixture to bubble and become syrupy, then add the lemon juice and the mangoes. Warm through for a couple of minutes, then take off the heat.

Spoon the vermicelli pudding into individual bowls, and top with the syrupy mangoes and a sprinkling of chopped pistachios. Either eat hot straight away, or refrigerate and eat when cold.

PISTACHIO, ORANGE ZEST + DATE NANKATAI

My Aunt Dina always has a batch of these tucked away in a stainless-steel tin in the kitchen. There's a considerable amount of tense anticipation around the table at teatime until she opens it and hands them out, and then it feels as though the world is put to rights again. Their texture is similar to shortbread, but it's more like taking a bite out of a sweet little sugar-spun rose and pistachio cloud. They're light, airy, and perfectly complement a cup of tea.

Makes **25**

100g shelled pistachios
220g cold unsalted butter
250g plain flour
50g rice flour
120g caster sugar
a small pinch of salt
zest of 1 orange
50g chopped dates
⅔ teaspoon ground cardamom
    (or finely ground seeds from
    10 pods)

Blitz the pistachios in a food processor to a coarse texture, or grind with a pestle and mortar. Dice the cold butter and place in a large mixing bowl. Add the flours, 100g of the sugar, the salt, orange zest, dates and cardamom. Set aside 2 tablespoons of the blitzed pistachios to decorate, then add the rest to the bowl.

Rub the butter through the flour mix with your fingers, and slowly bring the dough together using your hands. Knead it until the dough is smooth, but don't overwork it. Divide the dough into two, then roll each piece into a log shape around 5cm in diameter. Wrap up in cling film and pop in the fridge for 45 minutes to 1 hour to firm up.

Preheat the oven to 160°C/320°F/gas 3 and line two baking trays with greaseproof paper. When the dough is ready, take it out of the fridge and unwrap. Using a sharp knife, cut 1cm slices from the log and lay them 3cm apart on the baking trays (they will spread when they bake).

Sprinkle with the remaining sugar and ground pistachios, then bake for 20 to 25 minutes, keeping an eye on them. You want them to be a pale gold colour, not browned.

Remove from the oven and leave to cool before removing from the tray.

CARROT HALWA WITH
GARAM MASALA PECANS

(gajar ka halwa)

This recipe marks a milestone in my relationship with my mother. When I gave her some of the halwa with a cup of tea, she burst into tears. I was horrified something was wrong. 'No,' she said, 'but I think it's better than mine!'

If eating carrots as a pudding strikes you as odd, remember how good a spiced carrot cake is. This isn't too distant a cousin.

Serves **4**

60g unsalted butter
80g pecans
1½ tablespoons powdered
   jaggery or brown sugar
⅓ teaspoon garam masala
750g carrots, peeled
   and grated
250ml condensed milk
1 teaspoon ground cardamom
   (or finely ground seeds
   from 12 pods)

First caramelize the pecans. Line an oven tray with baking paper. Heat 10g of the butter in a saucepan over a medium heat, and when the butter starts to foam, add the pecans, jaggery and garam masala, and stir. Keep stirring until the jaggery melts and turns a warm brown, then take off the heat and tip on to the tray. Be careful as the sugar will be hotter than the sun. If you feel inclined to separate the nuts before the sugar sets, do so with a fork. Leave to cool while you make the halwa.

Melt the rest of the butter in a non-stick pan over a low to medium heat and, when hot, add the grated carrot. Cook for 10 minutes, until wilted and soft, then add the condensed milk. Stir regularly for another 10 minutes, then add the cardamom and mix well. Cook for a further 5 minutes, then take off the heat.

Spoon the halwa into bowls and distribute the nuts between them.

GF

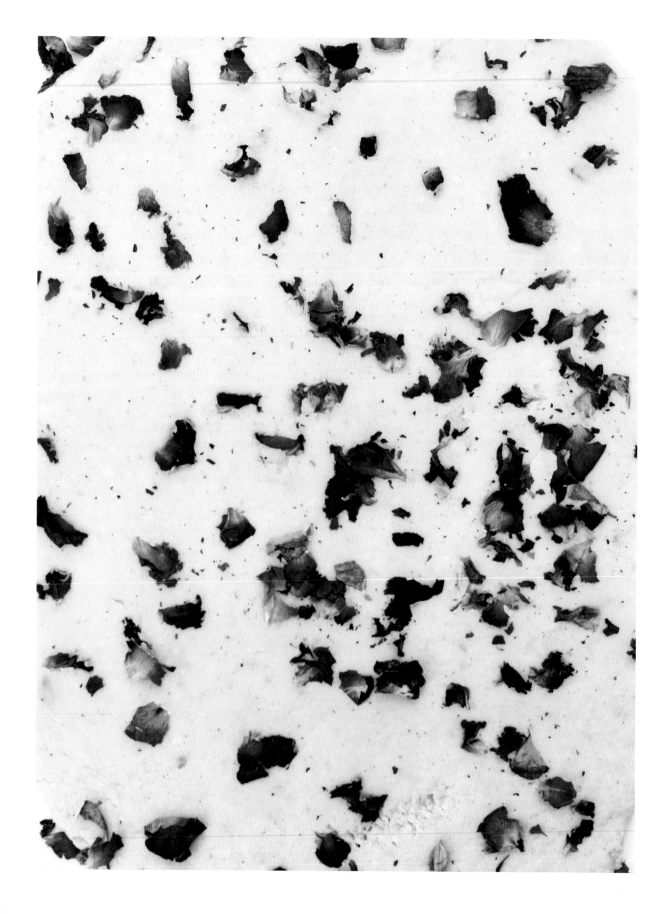

CASHEW NUT FUDGE

(kaju katli)

There is a secret to this one, my grandma said: you know it's done when the spoon stands up by itself in the mixture. And with this piece of advice, I have always had perfect fudge. This is one of the most highly prized of all Indian sweets, the mastering of which should qualify you as an honorary citizen of India.

NOTE: You will need a spice grinder or food processor to grind the cashews.

Makes 20

250g cashews
120g sugar
a handful of dried rose petals

Lay a sheet of baking paper on a baking tray, and keep another sheet nearby.

Grind the cashews to as fine a crumb as you can in a spice grinder or food processor – be careful not to overgrind the cashews though, or they'll start releasing their oils and turn into cashew butter.

Next, pour 60ml of water into a saucepan, add the sugar and place over a medium heat until the sugar has dissolved and the mixture comes to the boil. Then add the ground cashews. Stir to mix, and keep stirring intermittently for 6 to 8 minutes, until the mixture thickens. As soon as you can stand a wooden spoon up in the mixture without it immediately falling to one side, transfer it to the baking paper. Sprinkle the rose petals over the top.

You'll need to work fairly quickly now. Place the other sheet of baking paper over the top and roll the fudge out to around 5mm thick. Remove the top sheet of baking paper and leave to cool. (If you've got lots of sticky cashew left in your pan, fill with water and boil to clean it.)

When the fudge has cooled, cut on a diagonal at 4cm intervals, then cut on the opposite diagonal at 4cm intervals, to make diamond shapes.

CHEWY DATE + NUT BALLS

(khajoor pak)

These irritatingly addictive little balls are the backdrop to every cultural or religious calendar event in India. They can be made in minutes and stored for weeks, and are delightful to eat as a snack, on picnics or even to give to others. A food processor will make light work of preparing them, but if you don't have one you can still make this recipe by chopping the dates and heating all the ingredients (bar the coconut for rolling the balls) in a non-stick pan until they come together.

Makes approx. 14

desiccated coconut
250g pitted dates
1 tablespoon coconut oil
½ teaspoon ground cardamom
    (or finely ground seeds
    from 6 pods)
50g chopped mixed nuts
    (e.g. walnuts and pecans)

Before you start, it's worth setting up your rolling station. Tip some desiccated coconut on to a plate in an even layer, and keep a plate for the finished balls nearby.

Check the dates for stones, then put them into a food processor along with the coconut oil, cardamom and 1 tablespoon of desiccated coconut, and blend. It will take a few minutes for the mixture to come together into a dough. When it does, take it out and put it in a bowl.

Add the chopped nuts to the bowl and knead into the date mixture until well mixed. If it's a bit sticky, rub a teaspoon of coconut oil on to your hands. Roll into marshmallow-sized balls, then roll around in the desiccated coconut.

These balls can be kept in an airtight container in a cupboard for a month or so, but they're much nicer if kept in the fridge, as the dates will harden and taste like delicious chewy toffee.

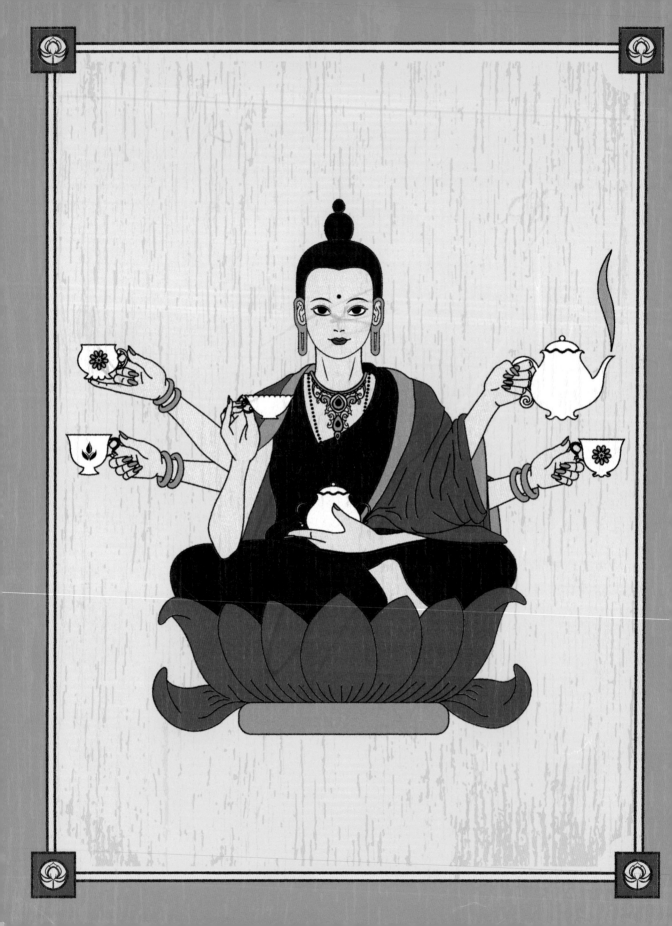

DRINKS

India has a very strong drinking culture. It's just not an alcoholic one. The relentless heat, which leaves millions cotton-mouthed every day, means the drinks business in India is big; in most restaurants, the drinks menu is usually as extensive, varied and exciting as the food menu.

Early in the morning, the smell of chai is always in the air. What one evening might look like an uninhabitable dusty patch of earth will have turned the next morning into a vibrant little chai stall with a crowd fighting for a sweet cup. The chai wallah, sporting a collared shirt and a well-groomed moustache, pours steamy ginger and cinnamon-infused tea from a great height in an act of theatre to cool the tea before it hits a customer's tongue.

There are more recipes for spiced chai than there are Hindu gods, but a recent discovery for me is the very special and delicate Kashmiri chai often served to customers in Kashmiri carpet shops and made with green tea leaves, saffron and cardamom.

When the midday heat sets in, only a fresh lime soda or a lassi will do. A common sight on most North Indians streets, lassi wallahs are usually found surrounded by big clay pots, busily pounding and melding yoghurt, fruit and sugar together. The fruit is always seasonal, and if you're lucky you'll be given a scoop of fresh cream from the top of a nearby bowl of freshly set yoghurt.

At home in London, I often use lassis as the vehicle for whatever fresh, ripe fruit I've spotted in the market – the sort that is bursting with juice and cheap to buy in abundance. Although the texture of lassis can vary enormously in India, I tend to keep mine simple, like a yoghurt smoothie, using ice cubes and Greek yoghurt to thicken, and milk or water to thin. The line is blurry between lassi and smoothie these days, and my mother often adds a couple of teaspoons of linseed and a banana to hers in the morning and has this for breakfast.

But come the evening, I'll always opt for a gin and tonic. Not only because it originated in India after British colonial officers stationed there started mixing the anti-malarial quinine used to make tonic with gin to make it more palatable, but also because it goes very well with samosas and other spiced snacks.

If you'd like wine with your meal, try a glass of sweet white wine, which will smooth the corners off a spicy dish, or a Chardonnay, which will work well with creamier dishes, like paneer. A rich robust red with subtle tannins, such as a Shiraz, will match bold spices in a dish, like a tomato-based vindaloo.

AVOCADO, HONEY
+
CINNAMON

MEDJOOL DATE
+
ALMOND MILK

PEACHES
+
CREAM

STRAWBERRY
+
CARDAMOM

AVOCADO, HONEY
+
CINNAMON

STRAWBERRY
+
CARDAMOM

STRAWBERRY + CARDAMOM LASSI

Everyone's favourite summer fruit , spiced up.

Makes **4 glasses**

400g strawberries
4 tablespoons water or milk
500ml Greek yoghurt
½ teaspoon ground cardamom
    (or finely ground seeds
    from 6 pods)
4 tablespoons sugar

Wash the strawberries, remove the green tops, then quarter the fruit. Put into a blender with the water or milk, yoghurt and cardamom, adding the sugar little by little until it tastes just right to you.

MEDJOOL DATE + ALMOND MILK LASSI

Almond milk, or 'badam doodh', is incredibly popular the whole of India over. It's a particular favourite of mothers to give their children as a soothing bedtime drink, and for many millions of us it spells nostalgia and comfort.

Traditionally it's sweetened with sugar, but I prefer to use frozen Medjool dates as they help to thicken the milk slightly and add a lovely malted flavour not dissimilar to chocolate or Horlicks. If you haven't got time to freeze the dates beforehand, add more ice to thicken.

Makes **2 glasses**

70g frozen Medjool dates
400ml almond milk
4–6 ice cubes

Remove any stones from the dates, then whizz everything up in a blender and divide between two glasses.

(DRINKS)

PEACHES + CREAM LASSI

A subtle creamy beauty.

Makes **4 glasses**

400g peaches
100ml coconut milk
500ml Greek yoghurt
3 tablespoons sugar or honey
a pinch of ground cinnamon
1 teaspoon rose water
   (or to taste)

Wash the peaches and chop into small chunks, discarding the stone in the centre. Put into a blender, along with the coconut milk, yoghurt, sugar or honey, and cinnamon. Go easy on the rose water, as all brands vary; add it little by little until it tastes just right to you and isn't overpowering.

AVOCADO, HONEY + CINNAMON LASSI

Travel the length and breadth of India today and you will find lassis of every kind, texture and flavour. The best one I ever had was from Blue Lassi in Varanasi.

This avocado and honey lassi borrows from that one. Creamy and rich from the blended avocado flesh and yoghurt, with honey, cinnamon and rose water. It's filling enough for breakfast or an afternoon lull. I like to use yoghurt which is a few days old, so it has a sour tang to it.

Makes **2 glasses**

1 very ripe avocado
250ml Greek yoghurt
250ml whole or
   semi-skimmed milk
1 teaspoon ground cinnamon
2–4 tablespoons runny honey
   (or to taste)
2 teaspoons rose water
   (or to taste)

Halve your avocado, then wedge your knife blade into the centre of the stone and twist it clear of the flesh. Scoop out the flesh into a blender and add the yoghurt, milk and cinnamon, then whizz together.

Add the honey and rose water according to taste – rose waters in particular vary dramatically, so add it little by little until it tastes just right to you. Blend, taste, adjust again if you wish, then serve.

KASHMIRI SAFFRON TEA

No matter how much you try not to get drawn into a carpet-buying trip by a well-meaning Kashmiri man in Delhi, you will probably at some point end up in a carpet shop. On the bright side, the Kashmiri tea they serve is a delicacy, rarely found outside of these shops, so enjoy it.

Makes **4 cups**

6 cardamom pods
1 tablespoon sugar
   (plus extra to taste)
4cm cinnamon stick
20 saffron strands
2 green tea bags, or 2
   teaspoons green tea leaves
1 tablespoon flaked almonds

Bash the cardamom pods with a pestle and mortar until cracked. Place in a saucepan with a litre of cold water, the sugar, cinnamon stick and saffron, and bring to a boil. Boil for a couple of minutes, then turn the heat down and simmer for 5 minutes.

Take off the heat, add the tea, then leave to brew for 2 minutes if using bags, and 5 minutes if using leaves. Strain into cups, sprinkling a little flaked almond on to each one. Serve with extra sugar so people can sweeten the tea to their taste.

ROADSIDE GINGER CHAI

Although I love my mum's chai, some of the best stuff I've ever had has been from roadside stalls in India (many with dubious hygiene credentials). The reason being that these chai wallahs do one thing and they do it well – they've perfected their game by serving up hundreds of cups, dawn to dusk, every single day. Their chai, often potent, and drunk while standing by the chai wallah's stall, is served in small glasses called 'cutting chai', i.e. a cut portion of chai.

While I don't normally take sugar in my tea, just a little in this chai really brings out the flavour of the ginger and spices.

Makes **4 cups**

8 cardamom pods
5cm ginger, peeled and grated
4 whole cloves
½ a cinnamon stick
500ml whole milk
2 tea bags
sugar to taste

Bruise the cardamom pods with a pestle and mortar until cracked. Place in a saucepan with the ginger, cloves, cinnamon stick and 500ml of water. Bring to the boil, add the milk and tea bags, and bring back up to boiling point again. Strain into cups, and serve with sugar alongside for people to add as they wish.

(DRINKS)
GF

MUM'S TURMERIC TEA

A health-giving, nourishing tea, best drunk when you're feeling a little under the weather and in need of a boost.

Makes **2 cups**

3cm ginger, peeled and grated
1cm fresh turmeric, grated, or
⅓ teaspoon ground turmeric
2 tablespoons honey
(or to taste)
juice of 1 lemon

Place the ginger and turmeric in a saucepan and add 500ml of water. Bring to the boil, then take off the heat and add the honey and lemon juice. Taste, and add more honey if you think it needs it. Pour through a sieve into two mugs, squeezing all of the juices out of the grated ginger, and grated turmeric, if using, with the back of a spoon.

GF DF

HOW TO MAKE...

Despite the rise of supermarkets and convenience foods, certain rituals and practices still give the day its rhythm in a traditional Indian kitchen.

First thing in the morning, my aunt washes her pulses and soaks them for the daily evening dal. Occasionally she'll take some to one side, place them in a thin layer of hot water and leave them somewhere warm to germinate and sprout.

During the day, she might make fresh paneer by boiling milk gently with lemon juice and straining the curds from the whey. They will then be bound and set in muslin and put under something heavy, like a brick, to squeeze out all the water, ahead of that evening's meal.

Last thing at night, fresh yoghurt is made in my grandmother's house. The milk is boiled, left to cool a little, and the temperature then judged with an experienced finger – it must be not so hot that it will kill the bacteria needed to make yoghurt, and not so cold that they won't be activated. The milk is then mixed with a spoonful of the previous day's yoghurt, and placed in an ancient steel pot to settle overnight. The cream that separates from the rest of the yoghurt is scooped up by the first person down to breakfast in the morning.

It's true that most of these things can be bought if you're short of time, but as with cooking your own food versus buying a takeaway, there is something life-affirming about doing it yourself. It will most definitely taste better too.

GHEE

250g unsalted butter

Pop the butter into a saucepan over the lowest heat and leave to melt slowly. It's important not to stir the butter because you need the ghee to form at the top while the milk solids fall to the bottom of the pan.

Keep over the heat for around 20 minutes. During this time, a white film will form on top and milky bubbles of the other ingredients will push through to the surface. When the bubbles are clear, your ghee is ready.

Take the pan off the heat and leave to cool for around 20 minutes, then delicately move the film off the top with a spoon or a spatula, and pour the clear liquid into a jar through a sieve.

Your ghee should keep for up to a month either in the fridge or in a cupboard.

BUTTER

250g double cream

Pure joy. Sweeter and creamier than the butter you buy, and made in just 10 minutes. You can make butter with any amount of cream, but the more you use, the easier it becomes, as it retains its own momentum in a blender rather than clinging on to the sides.

Pour the cream into a blender or electric mixer, and blend or whisk on a medium speed. At first the cream will transform into whipped cream and then stiff peaks. You might need to stop it and push the cream mixture back towards the blades. Keep blending, and it will break down into soft creamy crumbs. Finally, after 6 minutes or so, the butter will come together, leaving the white buttermilk behind.

Remove the butter and put it into a bowl. You can use the buttermilk as milk or in baking.

Add ice and some cold water to the bowl, and knead the butter under the water to 'wash' it of any buttermilk (which will make your butter sour and spoil if left in). Pour off the cloudy water and repeat until the water is much less cloudy, or clear.

If you want to salt it, do so now. Wrap the butter in parchment paper and store in a container in the fridge. Use within a week.

PANEER

 GF

Makes 300–400g whole milk

2 litres whole milk
4 tablespoons lemon juice

This recipe makes the 'soft' or 'home-made' paneer some of the recipes in this book call for. It's more like ricotta in texture than the harder cheese you can buy in supermarkets, which is more like halloumi. You'll need a fine cloth, like a muslin cloth, and a heavy weight to press the paneer. I use my pestle and mortar.

Put the milk into a saucepan and bring it to the boil, stirring frequently so that it doesn't catch on the bottom. When it starts to boil, turn the heat down. Add the lemon juice and stir until it curdles. You'll see the curds separate from the whey and form lumps, at which point, turn the heat off.

Line a colander with a muslin cloth and put it in the sink. Pour the curds through it slowly, draining off all the liquid into the sink. Fill the saucepan with water and pour it over the curds again to wash off any lemon juice.

Grab the corners of the muslin cloth and squeeze the water out by twisting the top of the cloth until it's tight around the ball of paneer. Keeping it twisted, put a weight on top of it to press it, and leave it in the colander in the sink or set over a bowl so that any remaining water can drain out.

Leave for 3 hours or so, until firm to the touch, and refrigerate until you're ready to use it. If stored tightly wrapped in cling film or in an airtight container, the paneer will keep for 3 to 4 days.

GARAM
MASALA

 GF   DF   VE

Makes approx. 75g

30g cinnamon sticks
20g black peppercorns
15g whole cloves
5g ground ginger
5g cardamom seeds

This is our family recipe for the classic 'garam' or warming spice mixture.

Place a small frying pan on a medium heat and, when hot, put the cinnamon sticks, peppercorns and cloves into the pan. Toast the spices for 1 minute, swirling them around the pan to toast them evenly. Tip them into a spice grinder, and add the ginger and cardamom seeds (neither of which need toasting). Blitz to a fine powder and keep in an airtight container or a glass jar for up to 3 months.

YOGHURT

 (GF)

Makes just over 500ml

500ml whole milk
75ml whole-milk live yoghurt
   (it's important that it contains
   live cultures as you'll need
   these yoghurt-making bacteria)

Pour the milk into a deep-sided saucepan and bring to the boil over a gentle heat. Stir frequently, making sure the milk doesn't catch at the bottom. Once it starts to froth, take the pan off the heat and decant the milk into a bowl to cool.

According to my mum, you need to wait for it to cool down to 'just warmer than room temperature' before adding the yoghurt. To gauge, stick a (very clean) finger into the bowl after 10 minutes. If the milk is painfully hot after a few seconds, it needs a bit longer to cool; if it's very warm but you're just able to keep a finger in there for around 10 seconds, it's about right. (If you have a thermometer, the optimal temperature is 40–45°C.) The milk has to be at the right temperature because yoghurt-making bacteria are delicate souls and the conditions need to be just right for them to thrive. If the milk is too hot, the yoghurt will curdle. Too cold, and the yoghurt won't set.

Whisk the yoghurt into the milk so they mix properly. Then pop a lid on the bowl, wrap a towel around it and put it in a warm place to set for 6 to 8 hours. I preheat the oven to 120°C/250°F/gas ½ for 5 minutes, then turn it off and leave my yoghurt there overnight. In the morning, you should have a mild, creamy yoghurt.

Put it into the fridge to set properly. Your yoghurt will last for around 4 days and, as with most live yoghurts, it will become a bit more flavourful and tart with time. Don't forget to leave a little aside to make your next batch.

CHAAT MASALA

 (GF)   (DF)   (VE)

Makes enough for
   a couple of dishes

3 teaspoons mango powder
1 teaspoon ground coriander
1 teaspoon ground cumin
¾ teaspoon ground
   black pepper
¾ teaspoon black salt
½ teaspoon ground cinnamon
½ teaspoon ground ginger

'Chaat' means 'lick' in Hindi, and that's exactly what this mix of sprinkling spices makes you want to do to the food you've just put it on.

Put all the ground spices into an empty jar, and shake to mix.

CHAPATTIS

Makes 16 (enough
  for 4 people)

450g chapatti flour,
  or 225g wholemeal and
  225g plain white flour
  (plus extra to dust)
½ teaspoon salt
rapeseed oil
300ml hot water

Put the flour into a bowl, add the salt and mix together. Make a well in the middle, add 3 tablespoons of oil and mix, using your fingers, until it resembles fine breadcrumbs. Pour in 250ml of the water, then add the rest little by little – you may not need it all – until you can knead the mixture into a soft and pliable dough, which will take 6 to 8 minutes.

Lightly rub the dough with oil (so it won't dry out) and put to one side while you get your rolling station ready. You will need a floured board or clean surface, ideally on one side of the stove top. You'll also need a rolling pin, a bowl of flour in which to dip the balls of dough, a spatula (or chapatti press), a frying pan, and a plate for your cooked chapattis.

Once all is ready, divide your dough into 16 balls. Put the frying pan on a medium to high heat. Take one piece of dough, coat it generously with flour, then roll it out to around 16cm in diameter, coating it with a little flour as you need it to stop it from sticking. Put it face side down on the hot pan.

Wait for the edges to colour white and for the chapatti to start to bubble (30 to 40 seconds), then turn it over and cook the other side for the same amount of time. Turn it over again – it should start to puff up at this point, so press down with the flat side of the spatula – and cook for around 10 seconds, then turn it over again and do the same. Check that all the dough is cooked (any uncooked spots will look dark and doughy) and put on to a plate. Cover with a towel or wrap in foil to keep warm, then repeat.

CRACK,
GRATE + MILK
A COCONUT

Smack the coconut against a concrete floor or the edge of a wall until it cracks, then quickly place it over a bowl to catch the water. Wedge the tip of a sturdy knife into the flesh and pry it out in chunks. If the flesh seems firmly stuck, bake the upturned coconut shells for 15 minutes at 180°C/350°F/gas 4, leave to cool, then try again. Each coconut should yield 200–250g of flesh. To grate the coconut, coursely grind in a food processor, or use a box grater.

To make coconut milk, put 250g of flesh into a blender with 800ml of hand-hot water. Blend for 2 minutes, then strain through a muslin cloth or clean tea towel. Squeeze as hard as you possibly can to get the most out of the flesh.

Keep the grated coconut, milk and dried coconut shreds in airtight containers in the fridge for up to 5 days.

SPROUT YOUR OWN BEANS

200g mung beans, or a mix of dried chickpeas, brown lentils and mung beans

Although you can buy all sorts of special equipment to sprout seeds and pulses, you really don't need it. A warm place and a bit of patience is all you need. They will take around 2 days to sprout.

Give the beans a good rinse in cold water, then place on a flat-bottomed dish. Cover with a few centimetres of hand-hot water, and cover with cling film. Poke a few holes in the top and leave them somewhere warm for 24 hours.

The next day, rinse the beans in hand-hot water, leaving only a small layer of warm water at the bottom of the dish this time. Cover and leave again for another 24 hours, and your sprouts should be ready.

Rinse, dry and store in a clean tub in the fridge until needed. Eat within 2 to 3 days.

DESEED A POMEGRANATE

Cut the pomegranate into quarters. Then, with your thumbs on the back of a segment, break it in half over a bowl. Most of the seeds should fall out. Ruffle the rest of the seeds out with your fingers, and repeat with the other segments. Remove any white pith as it doesn't taste very nice.

SUPER QUALITY

Dr Sodha

Himkabori A Useful Hair
Oil. It cures All Hair Troub-
les.Stops Grey of Hair.Pre-
vents Sleeplessness Cools
Brain. Increases Memories.
Himkabori, Is a Kabiraji Oil
It is an Ideal Hair Tonic

M.R.P. TK. 30.00

INDIAN HEALTH REMEDIES

Some of these might not get the seal of approval from the NHS, but they're used on a regular basis in our home and other Indian homes. Most of my family don't like to take medicine unless it's absolutely necessary, often plumping for natural solutions that have been passed down the generations.

FOR TOOTHACHE, USE CLOVES

The pain of toothache can be all-engulfing. When it strikes, reach for a clove and place it where it hurts, sucking on it until it softens, and chewing to release more oils. Cloves contain eugenol, which stops pain in its tracks and wipes out germs.

FOR CUTS, LET TURMERIC DO ITS THING

When I cut my thumb open while working at the restaurant Gymkhana, Chef Ravathji ran straight past the first aid box and into the spice cupboard, where he pulled out the ground turmeric and stuffed it into the cut, then bandaged it up. The bleeding stopped immediately, and my thumb healed nicely in 24 hours.

FOR BETTER MEMORY, EAT ALMONDS

Eat 5 raw almonds a day. Mum and Dad eat 5 a day, every day without fail, and Mum would campaign for me to eat them on the run-up to any exam.

FOR COLIC, TAKE DILL SEEDS

Baby colic can be a nightmare for parents. To help with it, a breastfeeding mother can eat a teaspoon of dill seeds or drink dill tea. To make dill tea, lightly crush the dill seeds and infuse in a mug of just-boiled water for 5 minutes. Add honey or sugar to sweeten.

FOR NAUSEA, SICKNESS AND SORE THROATS, GINGER IS BEST

Makes enough for 6 months | 200g ginger, peeled and cut into 0.5cm x 4cm matchsticks | 2¾ teaspoons salt | 1 teaspoon ground turmeric | 4 tablespoons lemon juice

My family is evangelical about these ginger pieces as a miracle cure for colds, indigestion and travel sickness. My grandma hands them out to all the other OAPs at her weekly meet-up.

DAY 1: Put the ginger in a plastic or ceramic bowl and add the other ingredients. Mix well and leave to marinate for 1 day. DAY 2: Put the ginger in a sieve over a bowl and spread the pieces out so they're not lying on top of each other. Leave to dry out for 1 day. DAY 3: Put the ginger on to a tray lined with baking paper over a boiler or radiator on low or in a relatively warm spot, and leave to dry out again for at least 1 day and up to 4 days. After this time you should have crispy yellow bone-dry pieces of ginger, which can be stored indefinitely. Pop them in a dry jar to be kept out of the sun until needed.

RECOMMENDED SUPPLIERS

Our supermarkets continue to outdo themselves in stocking more and more Indian ingredients: this year I've spotted fresh turmeric, curry leaves, Alphonso mangoes, cassava and okra in the fruit and veg sections of some bigger supermarkets, as well as jaggery, tamarind, 10kg bags of chapatti flour and chickpea flour in the specialist Asian section.

That being said, if you've got a local Asian supermarket nearby, definitely pay them a visit as there's nothing that compares to insider advice on how to buy the best version of what you're looking for. Otherwise, some of my favourite places to buy ingredients are listed below.

In addition, because spices and products vary hugely (especially chilli powder), every Indian cook has their preferred ones. I've listed some of mine below, although rest assured, I've not been paid to do so.

ARGOS [argos.co.uk]

Argos might appear an unlikely supplier, but they sell a non-stick appachatti, or 'hopper', pan which is otherwise difficult to source in this country.

THE ASIAN COOKSHOP [theasiancookshop.co.uk]

This shop sells and delivers fresh fenugreek leaves, fresh curry leaves, banana leaves, mooli and fresh turmeric, and delivers very quickly. Very helpful if you don't have an Asian grocer nearby.

SPICES OF INDIA [spicesofindia.co.uk]

This is an Aladdin's cave of spices, flours and pulses, and equipment like rolling pins and chapatti boards. You can even buy your own tandoor oven here. It's a proper one-stop shop.

SPICE KITCHEN [spicekitchenuk.com]

Sanjay Aggarwal helped his mum start a business to keep her busy. She is a superstar who grinds her own masalas by hand, puts them into steel spice dhabbas and even sews silk covers for them using old saris. Sanjay's dad packages them and posts them.

STEENBERGS ORGANIC [steenbergs.co.uk]

Steenbergs Organic is a family-run and friendly company committed to sourcing high-quality and fairtrade spices. Their range includes some of the more difficult-to-find ones like ground cardamom, amchur and asafoetida. Most are available in small quantities and come beautifully packaged.

THANKS

To my poppadom, Raj Sodha, a tireless pillar of strength, who always said that lentils are wildly underestimated in this country.

To my mother, Nita Sodha, for sharing her insatiable curiosity about food and teaching me to take pleasure in cooking it and sharing it with others.

To my editor, Juliet, for her incredible enthusiasm for this book and the food within it. For the loan of her lovely kitchen, shared passion in lime pickle and all the behind-the-scenes hard work she puts into making sure the book is the best it can be.

To my agent, Jane Finigan, for her intelligent advice, endless patience and cheering me along from the sidelines.

To John Hamilton, whose visual brain is just the best thing in the world, and to David Loftus, the best food photographer there is. Thank you both for creating a very beautiful book and making it so much fun along the way.

To the recipe testers extraordinaire, Hannah Cameron and Anja Dunk – not only for helping to make these recipes foolproof, but also for their incredible generosity with their time, thoughts, friendship and sense of humour.

To all those who contributed recipes, thoughts and ideas in any way or cared to share an anecdote or story: Nita Sodha, Harsha Aunty, Nanny, Dina Aunty, Pinky Sura, Aditya Bhakta, Hannah Cameron, Teresa Micock, Rhea Multani and Satish Warier.

To Ben Benton from Kitchen Cooperative for being an all-round wonder at the book shoots and a joyous man to be around.

To Ceri Tallett, the wonderful wordsmith, for so generously giving up her time to give the words in this book a rigorous grilling.

To everyone else at Penguin who helped on this book: Alison O'Toole, my designer; Caroline Pretty, my copy-editor; Ellie Smith, my editorial manager; James Blackman in the Production Department, who found me the most beautiful paper; Poppy North for all her hard work in the promotion of the book; and Anna Steadman for finding the loveliest plates among millions.

To all the fearless eaters: Steven, Lucas, Bia and Aidan Dunk, Conor McKenna, James Lefanu, Chris Chapman, Olivia Chapman, Alex Whitmore, Rob and Polly Gillon, Rob Kinder, Charlotte Jeffries, Harriet Slaughter, Matthew Maude, Clare Willan, Julius and Kelly Ekardt, Sam Trusty, Jez and Lou Cronk, Matthew Sharkey, Emily McClure, Andrew Bulger, Jay Maude, Barbara and Kevin Savill, Peter and Roubina de Winton, Anna and Andy Bickerdike, Harriet and Ant and Nick Gibson at the Drapers Arms.

To all the generous people who lent me things for the photo shoots; James Brown, Peter Cornish and John Taylor for the use of their incredible organic farm, Pollybell, and Carolyn Coxe and Jurgita for looking after us; Charmain at Crane for her cookware; all at Toast for lending gorgeous plates and aprons; and all at Dassie for lending super plates, bowls and salad servers.

And finally, to Hugh, for being everything.

INDEX

FIG TREE

UK | USA | Canada | Ireland | Australia
India | New Zealand | South Africa

Fig Tree is part of the Penguin Random House
group of companies whose addresses can be
found at global.penguinrandomhouse.com

First published 2016
005

Printed in Italy by Printer Trento S.r.l

A CIP catalogue record for this book is available from the
British Library

ISBN: 978-0-241-20042-1

www.greenpenguin.co.uk

Penguin Random House is committed to a
sustainable future for our business, our readers
and our planet. This book is made from Forest
Stewardship Council® certified paper.

KARAMCHAND KISHANCHAND

AHALIA

BRAND

LADY SODHA